Russian Ride

Russian Ride

THE ACCOUNT OF A 2,500 MILE TREK WITH THREE
COSSACK HORSES

Barbara Whittome

BXTREE

First published in Great Britain in 1996 by Boxtree Limited,
Broadwall House, 21 Broadwall, London SE1 9PL

1 3 5 7 9 10 8 6 4 2

ISBN 0 7522 0528 5

Map by Raymond Turvey
Designed by Roger Lightfoot
Typeset by SX Composing DTP, Rayleigh, Essex

Printed and bound in Great Britain by The Bath Press, Bath

A CIP catalogue entry for this book is available from the British Library

Contents

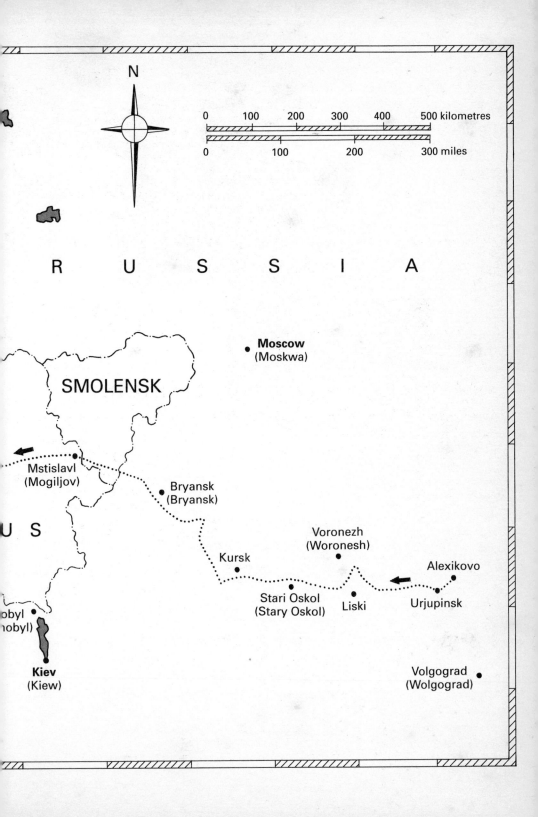

Acknowledgements

First and foremost I would like to thank my husband, Giles, not only for letting me undertake this adventure, but for positively encouraging it, for acting as essential base camp while I was away, and for finding and sending out the rescue party.

I shall always be deeply grateful, too, to Gay MacRae, who started the whole thing off by being kind enough to take me to Russia with her, and who (with her Borzoi dogs!) rekindled my teenage interest in Russia.

Had I not known that everything at home would be taken care of by Giles and Roy Cutts I would never have considered setting off. I knew that Roy would look after the animals as if they were his own, and I left without hestitation. He also tended the garden as carefully as if I had been at home, and so my thanks also go to his wife, Anne, who was forced by my absence to spend most of the summer blanching and freezing the beans and peas, redcurrants, etc. etc.

Although I don't suppose they will ever read this, I would also like to record my gratitude to the Myelnikov family, who welcomed me and my horses so warmly into their midst. They restored my faith in the reliability and sense of humour of the Russian people.

Without Richard Adamson and Alison Lea who accompanied me from the farm at Stari Oskol I can't imagine how I would have made it home; what's more, I have stayed friends with both of them! Thanks go too to my daughter, Katie Farmer, who travelled with me for a fortnight from Gdansk to Lobez. She had never done anything like it before, and I was most impressed by her resilience and lack of complaint when the going got tough.

We stayed with many friendly, hospitable and incredibly generous people in Poland, notably Marek and Hannya Borkowski, Krzysztof Niecko at the Sopot Hippodrome, and George and Alice near Szeczin.

Finally I would like to thank my mother, Olga Cornwall-Legh, for not making a fuss! I am her only child, I have never done anything like this before, and she had her eighty-seventh birthday whilst I was away. She showed a great deal of fortitude.

Introduction

It was only a very small amount of money, and as I handed over the cheque I had no idea how much it would change my life. My great friend, Gay MacRae, with six Borzoi dogs of her own and a deep love of the breed, had started a charity to try to get some food to the Borzois in Russia. It was the winter of 1992–1993 and the Russians could barely feed themselves, let alone their dogs. As an animal-lover myself, and as someone lucky enough to have a little money to spare, I of course agreed to help. 'There is only one condition', I told Gay. 'Next time you return to Russia you take me with you.'

I set about learning Russian, a language I had studied for about a fortnight when I was nineteen. I found a teacher, Patricia Sutton-Goold, who despaired of my total lack of interest in grammar, but gave me a language cassette. Being incredibly idle, the lessons soon drifted to less-than-frequent events but I played the tapes incessantly while I was doing something else – cooking, making cheese, ironing, mucking out, driving. . . .

I had more free time than usual because I had much less work – I teach people how to use computers, but when the recession started, one of the first 'luxuries' to go was training, and the demand for my services had gradually dwindled. Fortunately, I had had the great sense, fifteen years earlier, to marry an insolvency practitioner, so as my workload diminished, his increased. He is also a gun-maker and dealer which came in handy for this expedition, as he was able to sell part of his collection to feed me!

Fate had decreed that the next time Gay went to Russia she was invited by her friend, Anna Vladimirovna Shubkina, a biologist at the Academy of Sciences in Moscow, to go down to the

Volgograd region and take part in Borzoi field trials and hunting with the Cossacks. I accompanied her, and was allowed to ride the Cossack horses. On the first day I was only permitted to ride when the horse was tired, because the Cossack men needed to be convinced that any woman could ride, let alone a foreign woman. After all, none of the people I met had ever met a foreigner. And, of course, I could ride. When I was three years old, I had been thrown into the saddle of my cousin's mad chest-nut (appropriately named 'Dante', I recall) and that was it – I was hooked.

Having reassured themselves that I could stay in the saddle, I was able to ride all day every day for the rest of our short visit – in the end I was accepted as an honorary Cossack. I was really impressed with the horses – not large, but able to carry big men all day, and keep trotting. 'These have to be great endurance horses', I thought. 'Wouldn't it be wonderful to buy a few and ride them back to England and sell them to endurance riders?' The two sports of endurance riding and long-distance racing were becoming increasingly popular in England, France and par-ticularly America. I thought it would also help the Russians to let the world know how hardy their ordinary working horses are. I pushed the idea to the back of my mind.

Shortly after returning from Russia, my daughter Katie, who was on the mailing list for 'holidays with a difference', handed me a letter from Colonel John Blashford-Snell on behalf of a com-pany called 'Discovery Expeditions'. He was looking for people to join a scientific expedition to Mongolia. 'This is not for me, Mummy, but I thought you might be interested' said Katie. I replied, was interviewed in London, and invited to go to the 'selection weekend'. I have to admit that I nearly backed out on that weekend. Discovery Expeditions quite rightly tested us on initiative, leadership and communication skills, but I was abruptly reminded why I had never become a Girl Guide and why I had loathed boarding school. Fortunately I woke up after my first night in a tent and decided that if I did *not* go to Mongolia, then I would regret it for the rest of my life.

So in the summer of 1994 I found myself in Mongolia. I had thought that a month in the High Altai mountains, completely cut off from the rest of the world, might enable me to make some interesting discoveries about myself. There is obviously less depth to my nature than I thought, because the only truly valuable things I learned in Mongolia were (a) to sleep in a tent and (b) to pack a rucksack well. It was while I was out there that I realized that my dream of riding Russian horses home was perfectly feasible – the horses would be tethered outside the tents at night.

In late November 1994 I returned to the Novonikolaevsk region in the Volgograd *'oblast'* (county) of Russia, this time with my daughter, Katie and a friend from the Mongolian trip, Marigold Verity, with a view to buying two or three mares. I was thrown up onto a very nice horse – he was good looking, and had lots of presence and masses of potential. His name was a really Russian one – Pompeii – and I resolved to have him, if funds permitted. My long-suffering husband, Giles, who has not only encouraged this mad venture but paid for it, insisted that if I wanted Pompeii, I should have him as a Christmas present even if he was a stallion.

In the meantime, it was made plain to me that the Cossacks were so intrigued by this ride that some of them wanted to accompany me. This was great news – people who knew the horses and at least the first part of the journey, and who could help me in the unlikely event of bandits prowling round the campfire.

Gradually the journey began to take shape. There would be four horses, two riders (each leading another horse) and a back-up truck with a driver. I had already met the driver, Arman Aitkulov, a Muscovite in his thirties, whose family had originated in Kazakstan.

The following are notes I made when I returned with Gay in February for a final selection of the mares.

Here I am back in the Novonikolaevsk region. This time we came by car as Gay was not prepared for another 14-hour train journey in an overheated, airless cabin. Anna has found us an excellent driver, Nikolai Bezbatka, and we had a good journey as there was no ice or snow on the road, but it was no fun. The road runs virtually straight the whole way, and the views all round become achingly familiar after 675 kilometres. We stopped once for petrol, which took an hour. To start with, the attendant was busy filling a lorry, and then he decided to have his lunch break. Nobody thought it strange that we should have to wait. We were also stopped several times by the police, who checked our documents. I was rather alarmed at first, this never having happened to me before, but was told not to worry – it was because of the situation in Chechenia.

Nikolai is in his forties, with carefully slicked-back, dark hair and a few gold teeth. He speaks some English and I get the impression that he is ex-military, although he seems rather shy. Anna, on the other hand, is not at all shy. She is one of the only really efficient Russians I have encountered, and is constantly apologizing for the way things do (or don't) happen. She is only about five foot two inches tall, with dark red hair cut in a Beatles mop, and she smokes More menthol cigarettes incessantly. Her English is good, if inaccurate, and she never hesitates to use another word if the correct one escapes her, frequently resulting in phrases so mangled as to be almost meaningless.

Peter Krivov, from whom I bought Rada (a dark grey mare) on my last visit, was waiting for us. It had been arranged for us to rent his son's and daughter-in-law's (Andrei and Oxanne) portion of the house as we had last time. Contrary to my previous visit when she was rudely frosty, Oxanne was all smiles this time. Is it because the rent last time enabled them to buy a television, or is it because she is pregnant? She is about nineteen, and Andrei not much older, but they both look incredibly young. Peter, on the other hand, cannot be much beyond forty-five, but looks much, much older. The hard life here may account for it, but there is another reason. Some twenty years ago he had one or two vodkas too many – not an unusual situation among the Russians – but one which, in his case, had awful consequences. In his slightly merry state, he rode one of his horses into a building during some local Communist Party celebrations. For his disrespect, he was sent to Siberia for eight years and has not touched a drop of alcohol since.

The weather was foul on the day that we went to see Pompeii, the stallion, and to look at some more mares. The drive to the co-operative farm felt a bit like being at sea, but instead of blue sea meeting blue sky, we had difficulty making out where the snow-covered fields met the snow-coloured sky. When we emerged from the car the wind was bitter and it was actually raining although the ground was still freezing, which did not make for easy walking. Our visit was very disappointing. The weather conditions for the previous month or so had been dangerous and none of the potential horses had been ridden, or even handled. They had to be rounded up in the corral and herded into the stable, a process which left Pompeii rather excited, and the two mares were nervous wrecks who could not even be touched. I then found out that neither had been broken in!

Vassily Vadianov, who was in charge of the farm, wanted to ride with me to England.

While the rounding up was taking place we went to look at another group of mares. Unfortunately, most of the best mares were in foal, but one dark grey mare made overtures and kept nuzzling me. She has selected herself. She was also unbroken.

After some negotiation, I paid half the agreed price for Pompeii, the dark grey and one of the wild horses, the choice to be made by me in May. I also left money for the upkeep of the three horses, and half the money required for all the animals to be prepared – broken in where necessary, taught some manners and all to be as fit as possible for my return.

The following day we went to see some sort of official called Sergei Chulkov to find out if Vassily could get permission to come to England. Sergei's office was just what I expected: shabby and rundown, with an atmosphere that reminded me of schooldays and childhood misdemeanours. Being told to wait outside his office felt exactly like waiting to see the headmistress. To my surprise, we did not have to wait for more than a few minutes before being ushered in.

At first sight, Sergei looked grim – a typical petty official, unhealthy looking, and wearing a drab, none-too-clean suit, but I thought I detected a trace of humour in his face. As Anna explained about my ride, and how the Academy of Science was backing me to take good examples of ordinary Russian working horses to the West, Sergei's grim appearance gradually thawed into a smile. Not only did he agree to authorize Vassily to go, he picked up the phone to another official in Volgograd to smooth Vassily's passport application. He also announced he would like to come with us.

Sergei's reaction to my proposed ride was typically Russian, and therefore opposite to the average English reaction. When told, both nationalities at first look amazed at the very idea – then the Russians laugh with delight, while the English not only say I am mad, but spend the next half hour coming up with possible dangers and difficulties.

I am only really concerned at this stage with two problems. One is the EC bureaucracy and red tape, and the other is the notorious unreliability of the Russians. I have no doubt that Anna will do everything she promises, but will my horses be ready on time? Will they even be broken in? Will those Russians who have said they will accompany me actually turn up when the time comes? Having learnt to crank my natural lifestyle and impatience down a gear or two to adapt to life in a Suffolk village, I shall have to crank down another dozen notches if I am not to have an ulcer by the end of my ride.

I have brought eight 'kind' English bits (snaffles) for Peter to put on *to the traditional Cossack bridles – four for me, and four for himself. The local bits, while theoretically snaffles, are rusty steel and I have seen many horses with blood at the corners of their mouths. I have also brought an electric fence – the stakes for which, once I had wrapped them up, looked rather like the shape of a shotgun case. I anticipated trouble when checking in at the airport, but got none at all. The fence is to teach the horses not to jump out of a field.*

The horses I buy are certainly in for a major culture shock. Not only do we in the West pamper our horses, but the concept of a 'field' is completely alien to the Russians. The Cossack horses either live in a stable or in a corral, or are left to wander the steppes at will and are rounded up when required. There may also be problems with shoeing, although I asked Vassily to give them as much practice as possible.

From a British perspective, the animals in Russia are not well treated. The Russians are not cruel to them, but they do not treat them as we do. For example, we heard of a borzoi that had recently died of distemper – not just any old borzoi, but one which had proved himself exceptionally fast and brave by killing a wolf. Inoculations for distemper seem unknown out here in Novonikolaevsk, although they are routinely used in Moscow.

The life of the people is so hard here. They find they don't have the time or the energy to make the lives of the animals easier. But why is life so hard here? I am mystified that the people cannot organize themselves better: the land is extraordinarily good and fertile and I feel anything could grow here, but – apart from the Steppe areas – all we see are vast areas of wheat or plough. The country people eat well enough, compared with the townspeople, but their lives seem to mirror those of our peasants during the Middle Ages. Our 'lavatory' was an earth-box in the garden, and freezers, washing machines, hot running water and telephones seem either unheard of or unaffordable, although there is electricity. That said, our local electrician would faint on the spot. If you put the plug in to boil the kettle, blue sparks fly, and every time the fridge motor cuts in, the lights flicker.

Back in England I really got to work on the red tape. My first call was to our Ministry of Agriculture, Fisheries and Food (MAFF). I explained what I planned to do to the woman who answered the phone, and asked what documents would be required for the horses. 'You need a health certificate, which is valid for ten days', she informed me. 'But it is 2,500 miles. I cannot possibly ride that in ten days!' I protested. 'Then you can't do it', she stated flatly, and put the receiver down. I rang back and asked to speak to the most senior veterinary person, and was put through to Bob Davies. He was much more helpful and explained that, within three weeks of our intended arrival date, we needed to take blood samples from the horses, and have them analysed by the Central Veterinary Laboratories in Addlestone. If the tests were clear, then health certificates would be issued and the horses would be free to enter the EC.

Because I was planning to ride through Germany, I also contacted Mr Valder, Mr Davies' opposite number in Germany. The response was a fax and a telephone call: 'You cannot ride across the border, it is not foreseen!' (by which I suppose he meant 'it is not in the book'). Oh rubbish, I thought, if I can drive a horsebox across the border, I can surely ride.

My next call was to Brussels, on the grounds that the bureaucrats there must outrank all the ones in the individual countries. Eventually I acquired the name and phone number of the very best person to help me – Monsieur Bernard van Goethem – who I understood to be the Chief Veterinarian at the Commission of the European Community. He was wonderful, and talked to both the British and the German authorities, and it was agreed by all concerned that I could ride into the EC.

To get permission to cross Poland, all I needed was to pay US $100 (£66)!

It occurred to me that Russian, French and German might not be enough to get by while we were in Poland, and I asked our Polish-born friend, Jon Ryder to translate a few essential phrases for me. He not only did as I had asked, but also very generously gave me a copy of *Colloquial Polish*, which comes in a package with a book and a cassette. It so happens that the Gods gave me a good ear (although they did not give me the gift of application), so I can pick up words and phrases I hear around me while having no idea of the grammar or any inclination to study or do anything resembling hard work.

My mother is Swiss and I was born in Zurich, and I would have to have been deaf not to have acquired some grasp of Swiss–German, which I later improved by doing German 'A' level. I also went to school in Brussels, where I learnt passable French.

My next quest was for a list of farriers and vets across my proposed route in Poland and Germany. Here I must thank the incredibly helpful British Embassy staff in Warsaw and Bonn.

My great friend, Angelika Neuhaus was contacted and asked if she could find me the German equivalent of our Ordnance Survey maps, showing all the bridle paths. After two weeks it emerged there were none. However, she had been informed that there were many places we could ride legally and safely. 'Oh well', I thought, 'I shall just have to ask the local people as we go along'.

At about this stage I started worrying about the horses' stamina. Was I asking too much of them? What sort of food would I be able to acquire for them as I rode along? I contacted a friend of mine, Clare Hodge, who had just started a company, manufacturing vitamin powder for horses, and bought 40kg of the stuff.

Meanwhile faxes were flying backwards and forwards to Anna in Moscow. She suddenly decided that it was necessary to take blood samples from the horses before we left, just to prove they were healthy, and duly went down to Alexikovo to get them. In the meantime I tried to organise a courier to transport the samples back to England. This proved an impossible task – no courier company could guarantee that the samples would neither be left to fry on the airport tarmac, nor be frozen in the hold of the plane.

On previous trips I had always kept a diary, and fully intended to do so this time. I saw an advertisement for a Psion organiser, and I read that it boasted a word processor, a database, a diary, a spreadsheet and a calculator. More to the point, it ran on ordinary AA batteries. Giles rang the makers and, to my great surprise and delight, they gave me one free, together with a back-up diskette and a fax attachment the size of a couple of large cigars.

Another essential purchase was a video camera, which Giles obtained by swapping a Luger pistol. He had been much enthused by the results of my efforts when I was the cameraman during the Mongolia expedition, and was determined that I should have a camera for this trip.

By now it was the middle of May, and I had originally hoped to start my ride at the beginning of June. Although I had explained to the various authorities exactly what I was doing, my Russian visa stated that the purpose of my visit was to study the Russian language, and was valid for six months. My Belarussian visa allowed me to spend just five days in that country, but I thought I could sort that out once I got to Moscow. In any event, as Anna told me over the telephone, 'the border between Russia and Belarus had been destroyed, just for your benefit'.

Despite being as ruthless as I could, I was unable to keep my baggage below four huge bags, so I decided to go out by train. It was surprisingly easy – Eurostar from Waterloo to Brussels, then only about an hour's wait for the daily Brussels–Moscow train.

At home, in Suffolk, everything had been organized for my two old mares. I had rented some grazing nearby and just before I left I took them up to the beautiful field there. The goats had been found a new home with some people that seemed quite as potty as I am. I knew Roy Cutts would look after the remaining animals as well as he always has – he has been working here for seven years and is the most dependable person I know. The two West Highland Terriers had gone to live with someone they knew and loved. Giles would walk the remaining four dogs before going to the office, and he would also shut up the hens and geese at night. I had done my best. I could not bear to say goodbye to any of the animals. Would they remember me when I got back? I was determined not even to think about it, and I just got in the car and left Denston, but I never, ever, thought it would be six months to the day before my return.

CHAPTER ONE

The train journey to Moscow

1 June 1995
9:39am

I am sitting in the very modern Eurostar terminal at Waterloo, with my vast and numerous bags (including four tethering stakes) around me on two trolleys, having just said goodbye to my husband. It has occurred to me that, apart from the Channel Tunnel itself (the prospect of which I find more frightening than any other potential danger on this trip), by going to Moscow by train, I am ensuring that both directions of this journey will have been undertaken using methods of transport that were available one hundred years ago.

At Giles's insistence I am travelling first-class: after all the scares about rich foreigners being mugged and robbed on East European and Russian trains, he felt I would be safer if I had a cabin to myself. Looking around me, I see only pompous businessmen going to Brussels for the day. I am wearing jeans and a T-shirt and my 'expedition' hat, a rucksack and bum-bag. I bet I am the least typical first-class passenger Eurostar have ever had!

I had asked the Eurostar staff to arrange for a porter to meet me at Brussels, and indeed one was waiting for me as we stopped. As I feared, he was a Flemish-speaker, but he spoke enough French to get by. He left me on the correct platform with two trolleys, and about fifteen minutes later the Moscow train pulled in. I was in a bit of a panic, but the Russian attendant was extremely helpful after his initial shock at the amount and weight of my baggage. To my surprise and delight, my limited command of the Russian language has not deserted me. Now I am ensconced in a minute cabin, with the floor space almost completely occupied by luggage, as are two of the three seats Fortunately, the sleeping berth is overhead, so I shall not have to snooze on my bags.

No smoking, sadly, but I can have a drag at the end of the carriage.

We have just pulled out, bang on time.

After discovering – not entirely to my surprise – that there is no food on the train, I am faced with the prospect of forty-eight hours with nothing to eat except the little bit of bread and cheese I had pessimistically stolen from the hotel dining room that morning. I asked the attendant if I could buy any food anywhere, and he told me that we would stop at Aachen for fifteen minutes. Dare I risk leaving my luggage? If I don't, I shall barely survive as I have nothing to drink.

2 June
10.54am (Polish time)
I did risk leaving my luggage, but to no avail as the mini-supermarket at Aachen would take neither pounds nor dollars. I accepted the situation stoically, especially when one of the attendants came in asking if I would like tea or coffee – thank the Lord for the Russians' love affair with *chai* (tea). I remembered simultaneously that without food I was in danger of getting a migraine and that I had several large bags of peanuts. To cap it all, on one of my journeys for a smoke, the attendants gave me a glass of Hungarian wine – so kind!

Went to bed early, as I was totally exhausted. Was woken at 2.45am by a banging on the door – we were approaching the German/Polish frontier. When the customs men/soldiers came through, my face was scrutinized more thoroughly than ever before. They were followed by another soldier, armed with a mini-ladder, who checked the central heating cupboard, the loo, and all the empty cabins. After he had gone, I asked the attendants if that was the end – 'Yes', he said, 'we can all go back to sleep' – but five minutes later an officially-dressed woman came banging on the door wanting to look at my luggage – or so I thought. She only wanted to know how heavy it was – but when I told her I was English, she lost interest.

This morning I had a long conversation with a Frenchman and, among other things, he told me that one of the others in our carriage (a Russian or a Pole) had paid a huge fine because of the amount of her baggage.

The sense of unreality I had yesterday still remains, and is not helped by smoking and chatting in French to a man who I had originally addressed in German while crossing Poland in a Russian train. Have I become a 'new European'?

7:31pm (Russian time)
Going through Customs into Belarus, the officers were quite happy with my passport and visa, but one young officer demanded to see all my declared dollars! He seemed reasonably content when I explained about the hidden ones. This was money that Giles had concealed, at my request, in empty tubes of face cream, and then sealed. Later, when I went out to have a fag, the officer was waiting to get off the train. 'What is England like?', he wanted to know. 'How did you travel across the sea?' I explained about the Channel Tunnel. 'Do you know there are bandits in Russia?' I said, 'Yes, but there are bandits in England, too, although they are mainly in the cities'.

I had been a bit nervous about going across frontiers. One of the reasons for having so much luggage was the 40kg (88lb) of vitamin powder for the horses. It occurred to me only when I was packing it, that some official somewhere would be bound to query twenty bags of white powder in plastic bags. As it was, my luggage was never inspected.

The train stopped in a vast shed soon after the border crossing, and each individual carriage had its coupling arrangements changed, and then was lifted high in the air while the sets of wheels were changed. While this was going on, we were quite free to wander where we pleased, so before even getting to Moscow, I experienced that wonderful sense of freedom which I always have in Russia – of not being bossed around by petty officials with an overbearing concern for my safety. Here I can kill myself by my own stupidity in any way I choose.

I have just been swamped at the open door by women selling things and I bought a roast chicken, mineral water, keffir (which is a rather thin, natural yoghurt) and beer. The attendant then told me that we now had a restaurant car on the train.

3 June
9:10am
Gorged myself on keffir and mineral water before eating about half the chicken. Finally, I drank a bottle of beer and went to bed, where I spent another twelve hours.

I am now washed and nearly ready to get off, but I cannot bear to put my boots on until the last minute. The whole journey has been incredibly hot.

I have been staring through the window as the train clanks slowly towards Moscow. There are literally millions of trees along the track, mainly the famous *berioz* (birch tree). Telegraph poles also follow the railway, but unfortunately, many loop dangerously close to the ground and, in some places, trees have fallen on to the wires, which would explain why it is so difficult to get a call through to Moscow. There are also lots of *dachas* (country cottages) with vegetable plots. Almost all town-dwelling Russians have a *dacha*, which in no way implies the wealth that a second dwelling would suggest in the West.

CHAPTER TWO

Frustrations in Moscow

3 June
10:46pm
Here I am, safely in the flat of Vladimir Nikolaevitch Shubkin (Anna's father). The train, due at 12.06pm, pulled in at about 11:45am, catching me out – I thought it must be another station. Then I saw my driver, Arman, looking through the window. When I told him we were early, he said no, we were due in at 11:17am– it seems that British Rail is no better (or worse) than Russian Railways. We had to get a porter with a trolley, and now most of my gear is in Arman's car in a lock-up garage – much easier than dragging it all up here when it is only horses' vitamins, my tent, etc.

This is the hottest weather in Moscow for one hundred years.

Struggled for ages to fax Giles using my Psion. When I had finally mastered the art, he rang immediately to say it had got through perfectly. All well at home, although he told me everybody is convinced they will never see me again. After reading Robin Hanbury-Tenison's autobiography on the train, I had just concluded that my jaunt is seriously tame.

Anna Shubkina went off to work while I had my rest, but I shall see her tomorrow. Then, on Monday, I'm off to see what the British Embassy can do to help with getting the horses' blood samples back to the veterinary laboratories in Weybridge and visas for the Russians. I shall also need to check again on the veterinary requirements in Poland.

5 June
12:31am
Spent the day with Anna, reading while she worked for hours on the computer on her book about dogs. She is also computerizing as many of the pedigrees of the various kinds of borzoi as she can. Then off to meet Tariq, another Borzoi expert, whose other names I have never discovered. He is my idea of the typical Russian (although he is Georgian) – huge in all dimensions and with a flowing mane and beard in snowy white. He lives in the Botanical Gardens, right by Moscow University, where he keeps no less than fifty borzois (some of them being the Horty breed) and a few bears. Tariq was vastly entertained by my story of the Customs officer moving my bag to see what contraband was concealed beneath the seat and almost giving himself a hernia in the process. I still find it amazing that no-one ever asked why my baggage was so heavy.

5 June
5:30pm
I am melting. I have just staggered back sweating and exhausted, having battled my way to the British Embassy in the heat-wave, only to be turned away by minions and sent to the Commercial section miles away. I regretted turning down Anna's offer of Arman and the car. By the time I found the place, it was 13.05pm and, predictably, they were closed for lunch from 13:00 until 14:30pm, so I bought a beer and sat in the shade reading Russian *Cosmopolitan*.

More minions at the door of the commercial section gave me a pretty cool reception, but I said I would wait for the right person. Was soon ushered in to see Iain Kelly – very nice and rather good-looking. He was extremely helpful and rang me back later with lots of useful names and numbers. Unfortunately, they cannot help me to get the blood samples back to Britain until the end of the month.

Living conditions, even here in Moscow, are fairly basic by Western standards – the loo is between the kitchen and the bathroom, and the walls are paper-thin so every fart is audible for miles! There is some loo paper here, but the dispensers also have provision for torn-up pieces of newspaper. I have never discovered the etiquette – for what occasions does one use newspaper? The dogs' food is mixed with human-use spoons and the same meal is reheated and put on the table until it is all eaten. I thought I was pretty laid back about hygiene, but Anna gives our bowls to the dogs to lick out (and the washing-up water is not very hot). Thank God for my strong stomach.

I am staying in Konkovo, on the outskirts of Moscow, which is surrounded by parks and has a lake and a forest quite close by. It is quite a large flat: there is a sitting room, a bedroom and a study. As usual, I have been given Vladimir's bed and he sleeps on a sofa bed in the study. There is also a sofa bed in the sitting room, and I have never yet been to a Russian household where there is no provision for unexpected guests. Living space is at a premium – nobody would dream of having a spare bedroom or a dining room.

Like all the flats I have visited in Moscow, the rooms are all rather over-furnished and absolutely crammed with books. That said, all my friends here work at the University. Vladimir is a Professor of Sociology, but has now semi-retired and no longer works every day. He is seventy-four and a veteran of Stalingrad. I notice when he is wearing shorts that he must have had a terrible wound in his calf as there is still a massive indentation there. A couple of days ago, he put his special jacket on for me – it is almost completely covered with medals!

His father was murdered on Stalin's orders – I suppose some time after the war. It has taken Vladimir almost until now to find out the truth. When I was here with Katie and Marigold in December, he showed us a video and a book about the detective work undertaken by himself and two friends, in order to find out the truth about his father's death.

6 June
pm
Sent fax to Giles first thing with queries about insurance. Then I rang Andrew Carter, the Polish-speaking 'Number Two' at the British Embassy, who I hoped would translate my Veterinary Permission to cross Poland into English. I am to see him at 3.45pm.

I took the Metro to Moscow centre, where I changed some money, before going to GUM. This is a 'universal store' near the Kremlin. It is a magnificent building: a huge, arching roof covers a multitude of booths on the ground floor and on galleries above – a vast indoor market. I had first visited it on my first trip to Russia two years earlier, when it had been a sad, nearly empty place. I was pleased to see that it is coming alive again, with booths being occupied not only by Estée Lauder, Ralph Lauren, Galeries Lafayette, Yves Rocher and other luxury foreign goods, but also by shops selling wares that even the Russians could afford. I bought myself a few little treats – tiny soaps, fruit shampoo, a sponge – before going to our embassy.

Mr Carter came down and very kindly translated the gist of the Polish veterinary permission, wished me luck and vanished. I had no chance to ask if I could send the blood samples home in the Diplomatic Bag, but when I rang Iain later, he said there was no chance – even the diplomats were not allowed to send liquids in it. I have been given the name of an Irish woman, Kielan Taylor, at British Airways (BA) who might be able to help. She was most helpful – I am to find out what sort of packing the samples will be in.

Another coup I had today was that I was twice mistaken for a Russian. Two men came up and asked for directions. I seem to have succeeded in going native, which could mean a safer journey if I am not obviously a Westerner – synonymous with being rich in the eyes of most Russians.

7 June
Have been to see Nina Pavlovna Mikhalskaya, where I was warmly welcomed and well fed. I am so fond of that woman, and she was so kind to me when I stayed there in February of last year. She teaches English literature at Moscow University, so speaks English well. The Russian people particularly enjoy Victorian authors (indeed, academic life grinds to a halt once a week when *The Forsyte Saga* is shown on television), but this leads to rather old-fashioned speech.

She asked if I noticed any changes to Moscow since my last visit. I said I had – two in particular. One is that there is even more evidence than before of American presence, which is a shame. Of the other differences I have noticed, I only mentioned one, which is that when I sit in the Metro train, it is no longer screamingly obvious from the faces around me that I am in Russia – which it was, even fifteen months ago.

8 June
am
Going mad with frustration – I seem to be getting nowhere with getting blood samples to Britain, and I gather the process of getting visas for the Russians has not even started. I have the name and phone number of the Head of Visa section at the British Embassy, but no pull in the Polish or German Embassies.

10 June (Saturday)
8am
BA do not seem to be able to help with couriering my samples, despite my nagging. My best hope now is that a friend of Nina's will take the samples when she returns to London 'soon', but Nina cannot contact her and has to wait for her to ring. If she can't or won't do it, then Giles is asking our travel agent to get him a visa, just in case. Anna says if he has to come, at vast expense, then he must wait until we have gone down to Alexikovo to get fresh blood, which we cannot do until Tuesday at the earliest.

Fortunately for my sanity, on Thursday evening Vladimir found two Dorothy Sayers books and four by Agatha Christie. I have read all but one, so I hope I can find some more today – albeit a forlorn hope. If not, I must just return to trying to read Russian, a process which, although still very hard on my lazy brain, does seem to be getting easier. I am going to the Institute with Anna, and at least I can probably find some reference books in English there.

Have just made a cup of lemon tea, which reminds me of the traditional Russian way of making tea. Start by making a pot – it does not seem to matter if the water is actually boiling. You each have one cup – for some reason, it is usually only one cup – out of this pot. Several hours later, or the next day, you add more hot or boiling water to the stewed leaves in the pot. I think this process can be repeated three or four times before the old leaves are thrown out and replaced with fresh ones. It is hardly surprising that all Russians put masses of sugar in their tea.

So I sit here, read, smoke, doze and continue to wait.

Later
Spent the day with Anna – it is still almost unbearably hot (around 30°C). We went shopping, and I was amazed to realize

that while a packet of fags is 5,000 roubles (70p) in the shops, half a litre of vodka is only 6,000 (84p)! No wonder the Russians have a reputation for drinking.

11 June
There was no sugar for my porridge this morning, so I set off for the *Univermag* shop to queue, but after waiting at six counters, I discovered there was none. So Vladimir borrowed some from a neighbour and I did not have to go hungry. The fact that there is plenty of sugar in Russia does not prevent occasional shortages in the shops. I was told this situation arises constantly with all sorts of different goods.

13 June – am
Hurray! There may be light at the end of the tunnel. Kielan Taylor of BA will take the blood samples on 19 June. All we have to do now is to get more samples. . . .

Later
Maddening day. I went to the Institute with Anna, thinking it might be possible to GET THINGS DONE – but no. She spent five hours playing with the pictures for her book, then said Nikolai Bezbatka had a temperature and had gone home, although what he had to do with getting blood samples, I do not know. Anna smilingly informed me that maybe Arman would go to Alexikovo tomorrow, maybe the next day.

14 June
Another frustrating day. Arman did not leave for Alexikovo; he might go tomorrow. He will contact me regarding my luggage – I must get some clean clothes and check the hidden cash.

Before I left England, ITN had expressed an interest in filming my departure with the horses. I therefore telephoned their Moscow office and spoke to Julian Manyon, who wants me to let him know twenty-four hours before I leave Moscow.

Anna rang – Arman will be off to Alexikovo tomorrow with a friend; they have a car at US $30 (£20) per day but only for two days. Of course I am not able to go . . . but I knew that. Am I being too tolerant and not assertive enough? I am dependant on Anna, I know, but if this goes on I shall have to confront her.

15 June

Will I ever get out of this city? In spite of last night's thunder and rain and some thunder this afternoon, the weather seems hotter – certainly muggier – than ever.

Anna came round as usual and relieved me of US $410 (£270) for our tent material (an awning for all around the truck that we have had made, to give shade or protection from the rain) and US$110 (£73) for an in-truck fridge. The expenses are never-ending. I MUST be firm with Anna. I regard the fridge as a luxury.

Last night's news about 200 hostages being taken in Russia in connection with Chechenia (500 hostages according to BBC World Service at lunchtime) is bad news for me. Vladimir says Moscow will be dangerous (bombs on the Metro), and Anna says foreigners will be scrutinized all the more stringently, and documents checked and double-checked. At least all this delay should mean my documents are 100% pukka.

16 June

am

Another hot, but windier day, boring to the point of driving me totally nuts. I am being reasonably good about reading Russian (*Cosmo*!) and learning new words. I honestly think and feel I understand more on television than before. It is *such* a pity that Vladimir insists on speaking English! I know it is good for him, but apart from not helping me, his comprehension is very limited.

Tomorrow I am off to a dog show with Anna, who is supposed to fetch me at 8am – Hah! I'll believe that when I see it – Anna has never ever been on time anywhere.

17 June

It is 8.40am and Anna has still not turned up. I suppose she will want a shower when she does get here, and then we will be in a terrible hurry. Anna's driving has been the most frightening and dangerous part of the whole adventure so far. She has only recently passed her test, makes horrendous use of the clutch, and drives much too fast.

Later:
Anna rang soon after 9am to say that her telephone had got itself unplugged so she had heard neither the wake-up call nor her father's call. She *should* be here about 9.30am. Surprise, surprise!

18 June

Had a weird day yesterday at the dog show with Anna. Afterwards I went back to Tariq's with Anna. He turned out to be rather pissed, which was good in a way as when we finally sat down to eat, he produced some of my favourite Georgian wine.

A Finn called, (I think), Harry turned up. He lives and works in Moscow but speaks almost no Russian. His English is slightly better, so at one point I was interpreting between a drunk Russian (a lot more booze had gone down their throats by now) and an equally drunk Finn. Not long afterwards I made my excuses and left, as they say.

Today, Sunday, we went back to the dog show. At the gate of the park our car was flatly refused admission, even though we had a pass which had got us through yesterday. Various people, including a policeman, agreed the pass was valid, but the gate-keeper would not budge, and we hung around for an hour until Anna found a Seriously Big Noise who forced them to let us in. She told me later the correct way to handle these situations – which arise through a uniquely Russian attitude, where the petty official simply decides he chooses not to pronounce a document valid – is to stand firm, be convinced that you know your documents are correct, and then be friendly to the official concerned. Things got quite nasty today – the petty official drew up barriers and brought out a chair and sat on it. Anna eventually hurled her car forward and stopped in such a way as to block the way for all other cars.

The owner of the Champion Horty was dead drunk, so we took his dog, collected his prize, loaded his unconscious body into the car, together with his dog, two Irish Wolfhounds, three Hortys and Tariq, and took him home.

Giles rang very early and I gave him details for meeting Kielan Taylor with the blood samples tomorrow. Anna has just gone home to ring Arman, as we have still not heard from him. I shall behave like a spoilt fourteen year old and scream and stamp my feet if Arman has not got the samples.

9:50am
I simply cannot bear it – Arman's hired car broke down on Saturday and they are stuck somewhere near Raizan (about fifty kilometres from Moscow) trying to mend it. Maybe they will get to Moscow tomorrow morning, maybe not. I really think I am going to cry.

19 June
Well, after a bad night mainly spent trying to work out how quickly I could get to England myself, Anna rang to say that everything was all right and that Arman was back in Moscow with the samples. We are yet to hear the full story, but it seems the hired car broke down on the way to Alexikovo, with all the electrics failing, and it took them a day to get it to a service garage.

Anna and I got the blood samples from Arman's home (he was given the day off as he had not slept since Thursday), went to the Institute, re-labelled the test tubes, put them in a fresh Thermos, and added a letter to the vets at CVL and an explanatory note in Russian, in case of problems in Moscow. Anna then very kindly dropped me off at Sovincentr, where I handed it all over to Kielan, who seemed much nicer and prettier than she sounded on the phone.

Could we be getting somewhere at last?

I am now hoping to hear from Giles that he has the samples and all is well. I should know by 10pm as Kielan's flight is due to land at about 6pm British time.

10:49 pm
Giles rang to say he has the samples, so I can sleep tonight.

20 June
Russia is really not in the twentieth century when it comes to communications. The problems Arman had were that, the car having broken down on the main road to Volgograd [hundreds

of kilometres of absolutely nothing], he had no way of phoning for help. Having somehow got the car to a garage in a village, he then had no way of letting anyone in Moscow know what was going on.

I had not realised how few phones can be used to make inner-city calls: only two or three in Alexikovo, for example, which is definitely a small town, rather than a village and, so Anna told me, a Regional Centre to boot. I knew, of course, that international calls can only be made from Moscow (and I presume some other large cities), but this means that it will be much harder than I thought for those of us on the ride to let Anna know where we are and how we are getting on. Not much point having all these hi-tech Western gizmos if the phone lines only stretch to the next village.

21 June
9am

Had a super evening with Lyena Zharkova [a friend of Patricia], who made me talk Russian quite a lot, which was necessary anyway after Oleg (her husband) got home because his command of English is rather limited. Lyena's family originally came from Korea, and she is stunningly beautiful: aged about thirty-five, and with the most gorgeous black hair. She complimented me on my phonetics and said, as they walked me back to the metro, that she reckoned I really could speak Russian and would manage. As she is a teacher of Russian as a foreign language, I find that very comforting.

Oleg is a doctor. He used to specialize in gastro-enterology, but now works as a GP in the private ward of a hospital. He has just returned from Hungary, where he was finding out about selling life insurance to New Russians. It seems the Russian people don't like the idea of life insurance – superstitious? – so I suggested he just call it a pension! The banks here are so inefficient one can't set up a direct debit scheme (they are apparently quite likely to forget to transfer the money), so his clients will have to be billed annually. He thinks there are quite enough New Russians, and I pointed out that he could probably get quite a lot of ordinary people (like a thirty-five year old friend of his, who is dying of liver cancer) to pay, say, US $200–300 (£130–200) a year, which would give them a little something on retirement or death.

Either the mosquitoes are getting through the net nailed to my bedroom window, or Gulia (Vladimir's small dog who insists on sleeping on my bed), has fleas, as I spent one half of the night scratching and the other half trying not to.

22 June

Good news and bad. Giles rang last night to say both mares had passed two tests (and I think there are only two of them – for dourine and glanders) and that the EVA test for the stallion takes four days. This is a particularly important test – EVA is a sexually-transmitted disease which causes sterility and the authorities in the EC are understandably afraid of it. I was told that a Polish stallion arrived in England with a certificate stating he was free from the disease. He was not, and caused all the mares which he covered to become infertile.

The blood samples came marked with names of all the mares, but Pompeii's just said 'stallion'. I asked Anna about this, and she just said it was easier for Arman to write, but I have my doubts. Did they take the blood from Pompeii?

Am another US $700 (£464) poorer – unworthy suspicions are forming in my mind that I am being taken for a patsy. If Anna stops running for ten minutes I shall have to tell her that the supply of money is finite, and that we will shortly have emptied the coffers.

I had a lovely day with Nina Pavlovna yesterday. Unfortunately, it poured with rain all day and was very windy, so I have a truly dreadful cough today. Maybe that is why I am so depressed, but I must confess I am close to tears.

Later (11pm)
Am feeling slightly better. Anna arrived with Arman and *all* my luggage. After several anxious minutes searching, I found all the hidden dosh. I also have a medical kit (which includes Benylin) and some clean (and warm) clothes.

Anna also reported that she had spoken to a very helpful chap at the Belarus Consulate, and for US $120 (£80) he will extend my visa, no problem. She says it is the 'theme for discussion' – can't think why. I hope she will see the Russian vets tomorrow so our route can be finalized, then maybe we can sort out our entry point into Poland. I meant to ask, but forgot (as usual she was only there for five minutes) if the Russians' visas have been applied for.

Anna said she suspected I had a temperature – I denied it, but think she may be right. Probably brought on by fury!

23 June

Yet again, good news and bad. Giles rang to say Pompeii (I just hope it was his blood they took) has passed the EVA test. The bad news is (a) that nothing else has been achieved, and (b) someone may have to go to Minsk after all as nobody at Belarus Consulate in Moscow can confirm that we can ride over the border into Poland.

I have told Anna that the only thing left to sell is the house. I am seriously cross now – I no longer believe more than fifteen minutes a day is spent on my behalf – whatever Anna says. Meantime I am sitting here pretending not to be a coiled spring and reading my books and studying.

Was a bit miserable when Giles rang, which was not fair as he was so happy about the EVA result. I nearly wept when he said maybe I could leave at the end of next week! Laughed hollowly and said I'd be bloody lucky if we left at the end of next month.

24 June
lunchtime

Had a good night's sleep and woke feeling slightly less vicious.

Watching television now, and am amused to see business programme introduced by chap with long, silver hair and beard wearing jeans and a jean jacket!

Anna has not been here all day – she could be busy, but is more likely to be relaxing with Tariq or some such. She will probably be along later, but I really don't care.

25 June

Have just realized that my Psion will tell me the date and day of the week, both of which, judging by previous visits here and to Mongolia, can easily be forgotten.

I cannot watch television much, although I would dearly love the language practice, because Vladimir exhibits one of those irritating characteristics of those who live alone: he switches channels constantly and without warning!

Should be feeling better than ever – for over three weeks now I have woken naturally, drunk virtually no coffee and had very little alcohol.

Anna turned up at 3.30pm (having said she would be along much earlier) by which time, in desperation, I had cooked some chicken which was getting old. She apologised by saying how tired she was. At 3.30pm? She stayed for about one and a half hours, reiterating the difficulties with Russian (or Belarussian) authorities, at the frontier, for instance. In order to be able to batter them into submission, my papers do not just have to be correct but super-correct. I suggested asking ITN cameras to be there (instead of, or as well as, at Alexikovo), but Anna thought that might lead to demands for money!

26 June
Today I started reading *The Oxford Book of Exploration* – instead of inspiring me, as I had hoped, so far it has only succeeded in making me feel hopelessly inadequate.

Later
I was going to write: 'We seem to getting somewhere at last' – but I have written that before, only to be disappointed. I did go to work with Anna, however, and sent a long fax to the Deputy Director of Polish Veterinary Services.

I also rang Richard Lindslay, Head of Visa Section at the British Embassy, who said that as I had his name from Iain Kelly we could jump the queue. The possible bad news is they may want to interview Lev Zacharov, who is to come the whole way to England with me, although I pointed out that he would certainly be returning as he had a wife and children, and a job. All this in spite of the fact that, according to Anna, the British visas had been dealt with.

I met Lev the first time I came to this region and found him to be very nice and extremely amusing.

Have been offered (at quite a price) either a Great Dane or a pair of Russian shepherd dogs, which are ancestors of the Komondor dogs and look like giant Hungarian Puli dogs. Anna showed me a picture of one: it is completely covered with hair and it is almost impossible to tell which is the front end! When I say 'giant', I mean it: apparently a good-sized one can be thirty-two inches – the maximum size for Great Danes.

27 June

At 8.15am this morning I was wondering rather cattily how late Arman would be, when he turned up. I had neither finished breakfast nor applied make-up, the latter being (sadly) thought necessary for the day. No reply from Lindslay when I rang, so we went anyway. Tried again from a phone box – no reply. Went to the front gate. Eventually he appeared and said he had a meeting, so I left all the documents with him. Rang this afternoon as requested – he wants to see me and Anna, and all the documents tomorrow – I am hoping he won't need to see Lev, as it takes a day and a half each way from Alexikovo.

Went to the Belarus Consulate at 12.30pm, only to be told they open at 2pm. Went back with Anna just after 3pm to be told it had closed! Anna managed to talk her way in, however, and everything seems in order. I am to fetch my passport with the visa on Thursday.

28 June

Went to the Institute where Arman was baby-sitting Harpa, Anna's Horty dog. When I arrived he went off to buy a geiger-counter, which he and Anna feel we shall need when we get to Belarus, which was badly affected by the fall-out from the Chernobyl disaster. That said, we do have a map with markings to show where the worst of the radiation remains.

Anna had disappeared, I did not see her again until about 3.15pm when she turned up having been to the hairdresser. We all went to British Embassy, jumped the queue, spoke to a Mr Lovell who was very amusing – he even managed to keep Anna quiet. At one point he remarked that I had a lot of trust in these two young men. But he seemed happy enough – we are to fetch the visas tomorrow. Later on, however, I started to panic about time. If, as Anna thinks, their visas are only valid until 31 August, we shall barely have made it to England, so it gives scant, if any time, for me to show them around. Must ring Mr Lovell tomorrow and check.

I am still worried about timing. We are waiting now for the

vets' agreement to our route, and for some reason I am unable to grasp, we need the vets in Volgograd to agree something before the Moscow vets can proceed and, if I am not mistaken, vice versa. For even more incomprehensible reasons we are likely to have to spend at least two to three days in Volgograd before finally getting in the saddle. It seems unlikely, therefore, that we can set off before mid-July even if there are no more delays (and the Russians may still have to obtain German and Dutch visas, and possibly Polish ones as well).

29 June
Went to get my passport at Belarus Embassy. I had allowed lots of time to find it, which was just as well as I left the metro at the wrong exit and got into quite a panic when none of the multitude of streets looked anything like the one I needed, and nobody I asked had any idea. My visa expires on 1 August so, as I told Anna, we cannot afford to hang around much longer.

Back to the Institute, where I had coffee with Anna then set off to the British Embassy with Arman. The crowds were worse than ever. The Russian doorkeepers are quite savage at keeping their countrymen out, and are apparently unable to speak English. An hour later (by sneaking in through the exit and saving half an hour of queuing), I had the passports. Back at the flat, Giles rang and I asked if he could get Bernard van Goethem (the Chief Vet in Brussels) to fax permission to come into the EEC on foot.

Have bought a copy of *The Times* (for US $7.50) and read it avidly.

30 June
Giles rang at 10pm to say that he has had a handwritten fax from van Goethem saying something like 'It is clear the horses may come into the EC on foot – yes'. He will fax a copy on Monday.

1 July
Not a dull day for a change – Anna came round at about 12.30–1pm ('after breakfast'!). She apologized for being late but told me she had not wanted to rush away from her boyfriend of three years, Sergei!

We went shopping. I had thought just for day-to-day stuff but we ended up buying a few things for the journey including 2,000 Camel fags which were cheap. I did not have enough roubles and only old dollars so we had to find a bank with a forgery-checking machine. [In Russia, pre-1990 dollar notes are only accepted by certain banks, and then only in Moscow.]

Anna told me tonight that Lev is disappointed at the delay (who isn't? – I am going mad) and I must pay him about US $500 (£330) to ride with me. Is there no end? Whatever dramas and dangers we may encounter on the ride, surely nothing can be more frustrating than this inactivity. Giles told me last night (again) that he is worried, and that I am excessively brave. To put his mind at rest I pointed out that (a) I am not foolhardy (which he acknowledged) and (b) I would never risk the horses – which he also accepted.

It is just after 10pm and we have just returned from supper with Anna's friends, Ivan and Marina. He spoke some English, she did not, and I thought him the most dreadful tyrant towards her, their seventeen year old daughter and their Horty dog. He was also extraordinarily ill-mannered – he ordered his wife to bring tea (after we had finished eating) and then just helped himself – even Anna was moved to ask me if I would like some.

The meal was superb – melon, Kvass soup (Kvass is a drink made from fermented bread, a description I found so unappetizing I had not tried it until this visit, whereupon, of course, I found it delicious) and *shashlik* (kebabs) with salad, which included cloves of raw garlic – with one bottle of red wine. The evening was spoilt for me by a headache which threatens to become a migraine.

Anna's driving seems to be getting worse: she is nearly always in the wrong gear (on those rare occasions when she is not riding the clutch, which is ruined), always drives too fast round corners, produces wild jerks when she suddenly – too late – notices a pothole, and the brakes screech at every set of lights, with passengers and dogs thrown wildly about. She then crossly informed me this evening that her father had been criticizing her driving!

3 July
Anna rang to say there is a meeting with the Moscow vet tomorrow. I suppose it is progress of some kind.

Have calculated with horror that this month's delay will cost an extra US $683 (£450) for horse food and work. What if I find after a day or two that the horses are not as fit as they should be?

Later
Anna has just left – I may not go with her tomorrow but shall take the metro to the Institute in the afternoon to send some faxes, by which time she will have seen the vets. She suggested that I get more cash from my credit card on Thursday or Friday – so am pinning my hopes on leaving Moscow at the weekend. Is this another illusion?

4 July
Have sat around studying and reading all day, waiting for Anna's call. It came at about 5pm when she rang to say that the Moscow vets have agreed to do the list (route?) on Thursday. Hurrah? Certainly a thousand hurrahs if it comes to pass, but I am becoming an old cynic. Vladimir asked me if this was the final document. I said I thought so. When he enquired, 'Don't you know?' my answer was that it was, indeed, the final document unless the God of Bureaucracy found a few more that we needed!

5 July
Am literally in shock. Anna calmly announced this morning that I have to pay at least US $3,000 (£2000) tomorrow for the truck and Arman; that she wants US $3,500 (£2,300) for her work; that I need to allow US $4,000 (£2,650) emergency money for the trip [no vehicle in Russia is insured]; that I need US $1,000 (£662) for the vets; US $1,000 for Customs; US $1,000 for Nikolai to help us through the Belarus/Polish border; no less than US $600 (£400) for food and equipment(?); not to mention US $600 for petrol up to the Polish border. Have faxed Giles in despair.

I had asked Anna several times what to budget for, but she didn't answer – why wait until the last minute before producing these figures, which cannot be new to her? I also feel US $3,000 (£2,300) is greedy. She has done work on my behalf, I know, but only a few meetings and phone calls – I've already paid for her (wasted) trip to Alexikovo to get the first lot of blood samples.

When I go to the Institute she is invariably playing with the illustrations for her book on the computer.

Giles has just rung and has been marvellous – he says he will find the money somewhere and I am not to worry. I have said that I won't, but how can I not? Giles's first words were, 'She's stitched you up' and I'm afraid he is right. I feel really sick and dizzy.

6 July

Giles rang back later last night to say he has US $7,500 (£5,000). He also rang this morning – he has sold his Holland and Holland Paradox big-game rifle and is sending US $9,500 (£6,300) by Western Union which I can pick up at WU Sberbank on Monday. It's not quite enough, but I have decided to pay only half upfront for the truck, the remainder when we get to England.

Anna was late, of course, to take me to the meeting with her boss, Uri Prisheppa, to discuss the route and pay for the truck. I have no choice – if I don't pay in full they won't help; all said very charmingly, of course. Also, they are sending another chap at a cost of US $150 (£100)! Even so, allowing a bit extra for horses' keep and fitness programme, and if I allow US $4,000 (£2,650) emergency money for the journey home, then I am OK only if I don't pay Nikolai US $1,000 (£662) to come to the Belarus/Polish border (why should I?) and Anna US $3,500 (£2,300).

I have just calculated that unforeseen expenses (visits to Alexikovo, fares, extra costs for vets and Customs, paying for Lev, the truck and Anna now, rather than when we get to England), total US $13,800 (£9,140) – more than I brought with me.

7 July

Up since 6.30am and in a real state about money.

Giles rang – which I had not expected as he fetched Ali from the airport yesterday. [Alison Lea is a good friend of mine who lives in Denston, and had given up her job and home in order to spend a few months sailing to and around the Caribbean.] She seemed well, and I have asked her to ride across Poland with me – she sounds enthusiastic. Giles also read me a fax from the British Embassy in Warsaw saying that all was sorted with the vets, and that we have permission to arrive on foot.

Have just had a call from Andy Simmons at ITN Moscow – I rang them yesterday only to find that Julian Manyon has returned to London for a month. I explained all to Andy, and today he rang asking for more details.

It is just about 1,300 miles, according to my very rough calculations, from Alexikovo to the Polish border. How fit are the horses? At fifty miles per day that is twenty-six days, at forty miles it will take thirty-two days. I am paying the extra chap US $10 (£6.50) per day, and recklessly assumed fifteen days. It would be better to pace the horses properly and take my chance at having to pay an extra US $50 (£33) or so – although we will have to go as fast as possible through the Chernobyl fall-out area. At least we have a geiger-counter, and the British Embassy at Minsk said that the area was not bad; 'avoid mushrooms, fruits of the forest and dairy products'. OK for us humans, but how are we to stop the horses eating grass at night?

Other distances, equally roughly calculated, are: Poland – 340 miles, Germany – 300 miles, Holland – 120, and the last lap from Harwich – 40. That means that the Belarus/Polish border is rather more than half-way.

Later

Giles rang, and he has the new veterinary permit from Poland. I've asked him to ask our friend, Jon Ryder to translate it into English and the horse passports into Polish, when I get them and can fax them to Giles. They will also need to be in German.

8 July

Anna turned up at around 2pm and we went shopping for my journey. We spent about US $250 (£165), but that has bought me virtually all the food (save tinned meat) that she said I would need and nearly half the equipment and – I think – all the vodka for the vets and Cossacks. Must ask Anna how much more (if anything) to allow for the vets.

Katie said that her flat-mate Justin, who has had a lot of dealings with Russia, told her that it was typical of the Russians to keep adding to the cost of anything. I have said that I cannot afford US $1,000 (£662) for Nikolai to come to the frontier, pointing out that Giles could fly to Minsk for half that price.

Why am I so impatient? Here in Vladimir's flat I am not too hot or cold, I am dry, have access to an indoor loo and hot and cold running water, but I am still impatient to be gone to where I shall be exposed to rain, sun, cold, insects and dangers, not to mention having to use forests and bushes for a lavatory.

9 July

Giles rang to relate his woes of today: back from pistol-testing, he found 200 cows had been in the garden, after escaping from a field, thanks to a careless walker. The garden now has fewer flowers and a lot of cowpats. Then Mickey [the labrador] somehow got out and has killed four or five hens (the fifth being in shock and it may not recover). Of the remainder, three are in the henhouse and the rest have fled. Giles had to finish some of them off and in doing so smashed his best swordstick. To cap it all, he fell while chasing Mickey and has broken his specs, the spare pair (of course) being at the opticians.

What can one say? (Knowing our children, I bet they all howled with laughter.)

10 July

Andrew Simmons of ITN rang this morning. They are very interested indeed. They want to come to Alexikovo and spend a whole day with us. They want an exclusive, which I assured them they have, although I said I would like something on Russian television so my friends here know how I am getting on. He is also very keen on Cossacks wearing traditional costume, which I asked Anna to arrange when I was here in February.

Anna arrived soon after. She is not keen on the Cossacks wearing costumes (because she forgot?), and considers that it would give too frivolous an image and would cost several hundred dollars. She is now talking about taking a car (with Nikolai) down to Alexikovo, as well as the truck. Nikolai will ring me about this, but it sounds like yet another way of separating me from my money. . . .

11 July

Anna has just flown in and rushed off to the Institute, although I had hoped she would take me. I gave her another US $100 (£66) to add to the US $300 (£200) I gave her last week – that is for the geiger counter (US $30 [£20]) and about US $150 (£99) each for truck documents and medical insurance for the Russian crew.

I rang Andrew at ITN earlier. He takes the point about Cossack uniforms and seems quite interested in a Cossack display. He would also like to see the original films of me trying out the horses last December.

Anna also announced that she, Vassily Vadianov and Peter will come with us for the first few days until we get into a routine. Not a bad idea, but I wondered silently how much it would cost. She read my thoughts and said 'It is not a question of payment'. I suggested last night that we might be able to leave at the weekend – she sounded amazed.

I found an English phrase-book for Russians (dated 1957) this morning, which included the following gems:

'Please give me 10 shillings-worth of lobsters.'

'Let me see a lamb (squirrel) coat for the child.'

'Where do they run newsreels?'

'What youth movement do you belong to?'

'Tell me, is the weather suitable for flying today?'

All this, plus a thousand versions of 'how many widgets/ chemicals/tractors/bombs/square miles of steel/pounds of flesh/do you make in a day/week/month?'

Giles has just rung. What with scandalous exchange rates and US $300 (£200) fee for sending the money, I am now only getting US $8,000 (£5,300). I just do not see how I can manage, but I shall have to somehow. Boris Yeltsin has gone into hospital today (heart trouble allegedly, not dangerous) which means that the ITN crew is parked outside the hospital, along with the rest of the world's press.

Anna has also rung – it's OK with the vets, the visas for the Russians are in hand, and maybe we can leave Moscow on Saturday.

12 July

Up since 4am, worrying about money. Anna took me to the Institute, then Arman took me to collect Giles's money. First we found a bank with the right name but the wrong address. Then we found the right address but the bank had the wrong name – when we rang the number Giles had given me, we discovered the correct bank was twenty minutes drive away. They only gave me US $7,978 (£5,283), so another US $22 (£14.50) got lost in the transaction.

Giles has just rung. He has sold some pistols and is sending another US $2,000 (£1,325), which is an enormous relief. He has done a lot today – had the horse passports translated into German and faxed them, together with the original Polish translations.

13 July

Very busy day. I went to the Institute with Anna, and sent various faxes. I also rang ITN – they want to interview me in the forest here at Konkovo on Saturday.

Anna says I must give Nikolai some money on account tomorrow, and I suppose she must have her money soon. I may sound grudging, but I am. Even if she has spent one hundred hours on my behalf (which I don't believe for a moment she has), she is charging me over US $23 per hour, while the average wage here is US $50 (£33) a month. I am also expected to pay Nikolai around US $1,000 (£662) for two days' work and US $120-worth (£80) of petrol. I shall tell Anna that when I do the Karakorum trip [a much longer ride from Mongolia to Germany that John Blashford-Snell has challenged me to do] then I shall have to avoid Russia because of the costs.

14 July

To the Institute, paid Nikolai US $400 (£265) on account, and we all drank to the success of my journey. Before getting too carried away, I suggested to Anna a thought I had had in the night. We are running so short of time (not only I but Arman and Lev are also very anxious to get moving) that it occurred to me that Anna and Arman could take the truck and go to Alexikovo on Sunday and start confronting the local vets. I can fetch Giles's money tomorrow and my extended Belarus visa on Monday and take the train down with Vassily Terientich (the other driver) on Tuesday night.

This plan, which has been agreed, has the additional advantage of saving me a few bob – Peter's family charges the outrageous price of US $20 (£13) a day. Well, it is outrageous when you consider that it does not include food (which is charged at US $5 (£3.30) per person per day), there is no hot running water and only an outside shed as a loo. I can only be grateful that Anna and the other Russians are considered to be guests, so I only have to pay for their food.

15 July
Lessons to remember!
1. However wildly expensive you think it is going to be – double it.
    2. A back-up truck would not be necessary if two horses can be put in harness.
    3. Don't let any animals or other people cross borders – the paperwork is too much.
    4. Get everything in writing, especially exact costs and when to pay.
    The interview with ITN went fairly well, I think. I was terribly nervous beforehand but they were two nice young men.
    The rest of the day was spent rushing around after Giles's money. Then back to the Institute to load the bus, which turned out to be just a minibus, to my horror. Anna now has US $1,000 (£662) in dollars and US $1,111 (£736) in roubles, and I told her I would appreciate some back as I am US $100 (£66) short on current estimates.
    Arman and Anna went off to Tariq's for the roll of felt I had had to buy, which was to be used instead of a ground-sheet and/or as numnahs, [a numnah is a cloth placed under a saddle to protect the horse from saddle-sores], then to load all the junk from Anna's garage, then to Vladimir's flat to load my luggage.

16 July
At some stage I remembered my chairs and stakes, which were left in Arman's garage when I arrived in Moscow. Then when Vladimir got up he reminded me that we had forgotten the condensed milk, sauces, and dried fruit which we had stored in the fridge on his balcony. I could have carried those myself, but rang Anna. Fortunately she had not left and promised to fetch them, saying also that Arman had assured her last night he would not forget the chairs. Quiet day, for a change; I had a very bad

headache and slept in the afternoon. In the evening we watched a film called *Russian Business*, which was very funny. It involved a trio of unemployed Russians, one of whom is the proud owner of a tame ex-circus bear, who decide to run a safari to hunt bears. They find a pair of Americans and everything is set up using the tame bear, including blank cartridges. At the last moment a passing youth on a motorcycle stops for a pee in the woods and is scared off by the bear. The bear finds the motorbike and, having been a cycling bear in the circus, starts it, gets on and has a high old time, much to the astonishment of the hunters! The Americans end up inviting the Russians to hunt in America.

The whole thing would have been much funnier had it not been for their calculations of costs along the lines of '. . . $X for this, and $Y for that, plus of course $W for something else, $Z for somebody else, $A just in case, then add a nought or two because they are ignorant foreigners. . . .' All much too close to home right now.

18 July
I have re-done all the calculations – I had forgotten about food for the horses on journey. I think it will just about work out if I get US $1,000 (£662) back from the vets and only take US $3,000 (£2,000) for emergencies. I have just remembered that in the agreement we signed it was stated that the Academy would be responsible for insurance of the truck in Russia, so they have gone back on that.

A nagging toothache started after lunch – I have neither the time nor the money to do anything about it.

Giles rang – he is extremely worried about my safety. He hated saying good-bye – at the very end I think he was nearly in tears. Vladimir-Nikolaevitch and I finished the last bottle of Kindsmarooli [Georgian wine].

Vladimir has been so kind putting up, and putting up with, this foreign stranger, but I am bursting with relief at leaving the city heat. I am dying to move on to the next stage. I know there will be more bureaucracy and more demands on my vanishing purse but it's one stage closer to getting my bum in the saddle.

CHAPTER THREE

Back in Alexikovo

20 July

Yesterday was OK but slightly nerve-wracking. Vladimir Nikolaevitch took me to the Institute, but then Nikolai Bezbatka said there was a problem because there was no car available to take us to the station. Eventually it seemed there was a car, the driver of which turned out to be Vassily's son. Nikolai was too busy to come with us.

We arrived with nearly an hour to spare. Anna and Arman had bought my ticket and Vassily's a few days ago but, because Russian trains are so full and popular, it had not been possible for us to share a compartment. The idea that I should share with Vassily (whom I hardly know) is astonishing to me, but in Russia it is quite normal for men and women to share compartments and indeed there is nothing suggestive about a man staying in a woman's flat or vice versa.

When we eventually boarded I was in fear and trembling because, in order not to pay the much higher tourist price, I was pretending to be Anna. I had Anna's hunting licence as ID, but I look nothing like her, and I just prayed the *provodnik* or *provodnitsa* (attendant, there being at least one in every carriage) would not ask to see my papers.

Fortunately for me the woman in my compartment, whose name is Tamara, didn't want to swap places with Vassily. I was delighted. Vassily is over sixty years old, unfit and not particularly brave, and I felt sure that as a bodyguard he would be useless. Tamara is fifty, widowed eight months ago, and has a daughter and granddaughter. She would not stop talking, and was thrilled to hear about my adventure, although I told her it was a secret until our departure. She was made up to the nines, with a hairstyle like Madame de Pompadour, which all actually made her look much older. She told me her mother lived in Alexikovo, and I had a lot of fun imagining the contrast between this immaculate, well-dressed woman and the ordinary local people.

Anna and Peter met me at the station. Anna did not look well, and told me I had to pay tax, or duty, of about $225 (£150) per horse – ouch! Back to Peter's. Oxanne has just had her baby and is with her mother, and I am therefore in her flat, as previously. Went to look at Rada who was predictably chained up with a collar round her neck in a truly filthy stall. This is my first visit here in summer, and the whole yard throngs with millions of young creatures.

There were Borzoi puppies, kittens, calves, and a hen, duck, guinea-fowl and turkey chicks. We were told the turkey-cock had recently won an argument with a fox, although sadly some of his wives had disappeared.

The house is fairly typical of this part of Russia: small, square, and one-storeyed, with the yard almost surrounded by decrepit buildings, huts, and store-rooms. The yard itself is fairly unsavoury, with all the young creatures relieving themselves quite freely.

Time will tell if this village is representative of Russian villages as a whole. There are about twenty or more houses fairly well strung out, each identical in size and shape, and each apparently having the same yard surrounded by derelict old buildings. This is the first time I have been when there has been no snow on the ground, and I now realize that the whole village is several kilometres from the nearest tarmac road. I hate to think what the track to and through the village is like after a downpour.

After tea, bread and jam we were all ready for our 7am start – except for Anna who was still asleep. When she finally woke up and had her tea, she then insisted we had to have some soup before the journey. So instead of being at the Alexikovo vets at 8am it was 8.45am, and by the time everything was sorted out at the vets two and a half hours later it was too late to go to Volgograd. So another day is wasted. . . .

Back to Peter's for yet more food and a short rest. For some reason we then had to return to the vet's. On the way to see Vassily Vadianov [from whom I bought the other three horses] we stopped at a river for a swim, which was very welcome as it was boiling today. We saw two of the horses, Pompeii and Masha, the black mare, tied up in yet another truly filthy stall.

We had thought of buying a cart for the horses to take it in turns to pull, which would have two advantages. It would enable us to take some supplies with us, and it would mean that the horse whose turn it was to pull would get a day without a saddle, saddle sores being one thing we fear greatly, particularly in view of the soaring temperatures. Anna therefore asked Vassily Vadianov about the possibility of buying a cart, and then made what turned out to be the dreadful mistake of asking if we could buy a lamb carcass for Peter. That meant a ten-minute drive and a four-hour drinking session on the ground in the middle of nowhere plagued by flies and mosquitoes.

We are in real Steppe country here. It is not flat as I had always imagined it to be, but slightly rolling countryside, rather like the part of East Anglia where I live. I had always felt that Suffolk was noted for its enormous skies, but of course here the feeling is a hundred times greater. Another aspect of the scenery that surprised me when I first visited this region was the many lines of trees (*passadka*). It is not possible to be anywhere in this part of Russia without seeing several of these *passadki* on one horizon or another.

21 July

Utterly miserable, depressing day. Up at 4.15am, tried to get Anna going, finally left at 5.40am. We made it to Volgograd by 9.45am (instead of 8 as I had hoped). The first vet (who had apparently earlier said 'At last somebody recognizes the value of our working horses') was quite happy to sign our documents. The second vet we needed to see wanted some piffling form to say they must not be inoculated against Anthrax! Back to the first vet, who waited for the other vet to return from lunch and told him not to be so silly. We returned to the second vet, who decided after keeping us hanging round for two hours or so that he would give us one document but not another.

By now it was 3.10pm. We went to Customs (normally open until 5pm) but of course today they had shut at 3pm. . . .

I became very angry and depressed and asked Anna what was the point in trying to get all these documents if (a) people could

stonewall us and refuse to issue them and (b) any person with
any kind of authority who chose to challenge us could refuse to
accept the documents as valid.

We got back at 9.30pm, all exhausted. Andrei and Arman had
shared the driving and they both deserve a medal, but Andrei's
driving caused me several near heart attacks by driving at great
speed only inches away from the car in front. I am well fed and
tired now, but pissed off with all things Russian. Why are they so
lazy? So dirty? How can they let themselves be ruled by these
fucking bureaucrats? The men are so idle I was surprised to discover while browsing in the dictionary the phrase 'Idleness is the
mother (root) of all evil'.

23 July

In the evening one of the locals, Ura Kabil, who has a magnificent
Orlov stallion, came round and gave me a ride on his motorbike,
and even made me drive it. Then we went off to look at a cart,
which I liked and so did everyone else. Ura was our driver on my
first ever visit here with Gay MacRae, and it was he who pre-
sented me with the Cossack whip and Cossack bridle at that
time.

The whip had been ceremonially given to me, I think in recog-
nition of the fact that I had not fallen off, even though I was a
woman and a foreigner to boot. I had been told 'Cossacks use
these whips to keep their wives in order', so I immediately said,
'Excellent, this means I shall now have a very obedient husband'.
The Russian country society is so male-dominated that it took
several seconds for these men to grasp what I had said, but when
they did they laughed till they wept.

On that same visit we had struck a bargain. They would give
me a Cossack bridle in exchange for an English one, and they
would also make two fur hats (a fox fur for me and a beaver fur
for Giles) in exchange for an English saddle. The fox one I had
received last year, but the beaver one had not been ready. I did
get Giles's beaver hat this time, but Nikolai cannot have paid any
attention to the measurements I sent or, more likely, Anna never
passed on the letter I so laboriously wrote, as it fits me perfectly,
which means it will be far too small for Giles.

Back at Peter's, the women had spent most of the day preparing
a delicious supper. A great deal of alcohol was drunk, especially

by another Ura (who had arrived pissed) and who had to be helped on to his horse at midnight. We were all a little worried about him as, although he is an excellent horseman, he is apparently inclined to make his horses do crazy things when in his cups.

Amid much ragging, I persuaded Ura to agree that if I took him to England he would give me his magnificent Orlov stallion – we even shook hands on it! Anna told me this morning that he has not been home since Friday night and is presumed to be still drinking somewhere, so I fear he has forgotten our bargain, although Nadezhda told me that a handshake is binding.

Last night I finally discovered why I find these people so hard to understand – every other word is a swear word. Having learned two, I now hear them all the time and am finding it much easier.

Went to work on Rada this morning. She has no manners and won't stand still to be tacked up, and Peter told me I had to mount very quickly. However, she went readily enough, once I had made it clear that we were not going to turn for home after three minutes, and indeed wanted to trot nearly all the time. It was a bit hot, though, and I turned for home after about twenty minutes because we were surrounded by a cloud of horseflies. This makes me more determined than ever to get up at 4am every day, feed the horses and ourselves immediately, and set off before 5am. We can ride for about four or five hours, then rest in the heat of the day, and do another three hours or so in the evening.

The conditions all the animals are kept in still upsets me greatly. I should say Peter is a very kind man by any standards, and certainly by local ones, but why can't he muck his animals out, even once a week? Prince, the borzoi that was given to Peter by a friend in Moscow, is chained up for twenty-three and a half hours a day, and whines incessantly. I can't blame him as he is tied up near the earth box, which stinks in this heat. The new guard dog, a Great Dane, and the other borzois have not, as far as I have seen, been out of their kennels since I arrived here. Only the female borzoi and her three pups have the freedom of the yard.

Ura Kabil reappeared this afternoon, and has apparently found the right people to smooth the path for vet and customs documents.

Much flirting takes place all the time, rather crude flirting, it must be said. It is rather surprising, though, that these thirty year olds should flirt so naturally with us wrinklies. I taught Anna our phrase 'all mouth and no trousers' and she was much amused, but privately I feel Ura is a bit more dangerous than that. He is quite attractive physically, tall, dark and slim with incredibly blue eyes, but I have seen him at home – he is not only a drinker but a bully.

24 July
Success at last! This morning we finally got the remainder of the papers we need.

Tonight it is planned that I go to Vassily and spend tomorrow riding the three horses from his farm to here. They will then get one day off and we hope to leave at 5am in two days' time.

I have phoned ITN – Andrew Simmons told me that Giles had been on the phone asking if ITN had heard anything. I am to ring tomorrow night to confirm the departure and to get the registration number of their truck. It is to be a Russian crew and they will stay at the cockroach-ridden hotel in Alexikovo. I told Andrew that the Cossacks intend to put on a display of horsemanship, so would the TV crew please bring vodka and western fags.

11pm
It is still so hot that I am lying on the bed covered by a sheet. They are so kind. Tatiana wanted to give me their bed because this room is so smoky. They had been given no warning of our arrival. We just turned up and announced we would be taking the horses tomorrow, but still I am made royally welcome.

25 July
Everything was so strange, I found it hard to sleep last night. Another reason was, I think, the overwhelming stench of excrement. There are approximately thirty white ducks, three Muscovies, (both kinds with loads of babies), dozens of young hens, a baby goat, a cow tied to an old iron bedstead, nine pigs (in a sty), three horses (including my two) and seven dogs (five in kennels, two running free) – all in an area about 300 square yards, and apparently nothing is ever mucked out. In addition, the earth box is full, which is why I had my morning pee on the verge.

We finally set off early and had a very pleasant ride. It was only when we met Arman and Vassily a couple of hours later that I realized Pompeii, (whom I was riding), was all bloody on his stomach from gadfly bites. The next two hours were a nightmare, gadflies all around us, especially on Pompeii and especially on his private parts. We could not stop for a rest – we tried but the flies were even worse, and Pompeii kept trying to lie down. Eventually we escaped them.

We had been told it was sixty kilometres to Peter's, but I reckon that by cutting across the steppe it was only about fifty (a little over thirty miles). We only walked, except when Pompeii got left too far behind when we trotted to catch up. I am a bit worried about his stamina, but maybe he felt the heat more than the mares.

For the last five kilometres or so I announced I would ride bareback, so Vassily Vadianov did too. Pompeii has a rather prominent spine, so I don't think I'll ever be able to have sex again!

The base of my spine hurts from Pompeii's bony spine, the inside of my calves are slightly bruised and raw, and my thigh muscles will hurt tomorrow, but I don't care. At last I am back on a horse, in the fresh air, and on Thursday morning we are due to leave.

26 July

Time maybe for a description of these people's houses. The kitchen, approached through a sort of porch or anteroom, is pretty standard, about 8ft x 6ft. If there is a sink it is used for washing bodies and teeth as well as washing up, so privacy is a problem. As well as an electric oven for summer preserving, there is a solid-fuel stove there, and large pipes go all round the house keeping it really warm in winter. This is also the room used as a sitting room. Additional rooms tend to consist of a main bedroom and a sitting room, with possibly a third small room. These rooms are all very sparsely furnished, with a sofa or bed, and a desk or table, illumination being provided by a bare bulb hanging from the middle of the ceiling. The wallpaper is usually patterned and the curtains are net and incorporate a fair amount of glitter, usually clashing with the design of the carpet. The carpet is usually a cheap, colourful rug laid on painted floorboards, although in some cases it is a piece of fitted carpet just laid flat and folded if it encounters a piece of furniture.

Rugs of varying designs are also often to be seen on the walls and are sometimes very twee pictures of kittens – surprising in a country where there is no room for sentiment when it comes to animals. There are absolutely no books, or even magazines or newspapers. This contrasts with the flats in Moscow that I have visited, which are usually over-furnished and crammed with books.

The food in summer is good and usually soups and salads with salami or meat. Unfortunately the meat seems always to be boiled into a glutinous mass, with one glorious exception when we had kebabs. These people are also fond of fat – we were offered a plateful of pork fat last night, which was eaten with relish by all except me. Unless the food is liquid there are no individual plates, you just grab a fork or spoon and dip into whatever takes your fancy.

It is the women who do all the work. At the moment they are frantically preserving everything including my favourite tomatoes which are pickled with boiling water, salt, sugar and herbs. What I cannot understand is why they are so fat by the time they are thirty, while the men remain slim and trim despite their apparent lack of activity. The women wear multi-coloured nylon dresses and the favourite colours seem to be purple and orange, and I have yet to see a woman in trousers. The men wear T-shirts, trousers and plimsolls, and everyone has gold teeth.

In winter the done thing is to take your boots off as you enter the house, there is always a good supply of spare slippers for you to put on. In summer you take off your shoes or sandals and go barefoot about the house. Again this makes sense, especially when the ground all around the house is full of animal droppings. However, the Russians seem completely unprepared for wet weather: they have warm coats or jackets, hats and boots but no waterproof ones.

I still get angry at the filthiness and untidiness of these people. I know theirs is a huge country but yesterday, for example, even in the middle of the steppe we came across great loops of wire and piles of rubble lying in the grass. The Swiss part of me is especially offended.

As you drive around towns you never see a freshly-painted house, or a tidy garden – those that are not bare earth yards are completely choked with weeds. When I went to Vassily and Tatiana's house, Anna told me they were shocked that an English person should see how they live. I was surprised that they were aware of the comparison in lifestyles, and said so – Anna said the reason is that this region was very rich and bountiful before the revolution, since when successive communist governments have tried very hard to destroy the Cossacks. I fail to see any real difference between Fascism and Communism.

Anna also pointed out that the women in this region are much more independent and sporty (it seems they can ride, but I have never seen one on horseback) than elsewhere in Russia, as I would see on our travels.

Nobody in Russia has yet learned the art of dyeing hair: it is always screamingly obvious and, as often as not, has caused the hair to have the consistency of straw. I was a bit shaken to find that Tatiana, with several gold teeth, several teeth missing, straw-like carrot-coloured hair, who is buxom and seriously middle-aged, is trying for a baby – she is thirty-two.

Still no answer from ITN at 9am, so I rang Simon (the cameraman) at home. He thinks the crew is ready to leave today, but did not know the number of their car, only that it is a red Lada, which is no help here! The reason he and Andrew are not coming is that Yeltsin has had another heart attack – rumours abound that he won't live.

Oleg (a boy of about fifteen who was due to ride as far as the Belarussian/Polish border) can't come after all because he has got a job so, after speaking to ITN, we went to the house of Ura, Vassily Vadianov's half-brother. He has agreed to come as far as the Polish border. In what other country could you find an allegedly working man, with a wife and children, available to drop everything and agree to be ready for a 4am departure tomorrow?

After lunch I paid Lev US $400 (£265); I shall have to pay Ura US $300 (£200) at the border. Also paid Peter for the tack, the costs for Rada's extra food and keep during the two-month delay, plus US $460 (£305) for bed and board for all – outrageous considering the conditions and the fact that we provided a whole lamb!

It started raining later, and soon it was pouring down. The ITN crew turned up, and eventually we ate at about 9 or 9.30pm, having decided not to wait for Lev. A lot of vodka was drunk by most!

CHAPTER FOUR

Off at Last

27 July – DAY 1

It rained all night and because of hanging round for various activities (including the television crew disappearing for nearly three hours in search of Cossack costumes) we didn't leave until noon. We wasted a lot of time and energy posing, galloping about and showing off to the cameras, and then did about sixty or seventy kilometres. The horses went well and we were just walking once the cameras had gone.

I am amazed that after all this time, the planning, expense and, most of all, the waiting, I did not really feel any sense of elation or achievement when we did finally set off. I think one reason may be that I have in no sense been in control – Anna has been rushing about being bossy and Peter has decided on the route and the place for our first night's stop. Delighted to be back in the saddle, although I have got some rather nasty (and bloody) saddle sores.

Because of the late start we did not arrive at the campsite until about 9pm. We then had to tether the horses and feed them, put up the car tent (a sort of awning) and I had to put up mine. It is now 11pm, and supper is still not ready so I have gone to bed with only a slice of bread and salami. Anna is in a foul mood for some reason, shouting at my two drivers and swearing when everything does not go her way. I shall be pleased to get rid of her.

In the end four of us rode – Lev, me, Ura Kabil, and Ura Vadianov (Vassily's brother). The latter, having said he would come to the Polish border, then decided he wanted more than the US $300 (£200) on offer – he wanted US $1,000 (£662). I told Anna to tell him to forget it. The last I heard was that he would ride with us for a few days for the fun of it then bugger off when he felt like it.

We had hardly been riding for more than three hours before a policeman on a scooter stopped and wanted to know where we were going. I still don't think he believed us when we said to England, but we all had a lot of fun trying to convince him.

Soon after that we passed through Uryupinsk (a fairly large town where we had got the final document from Customs), after which we climbed quite a steep hill and are now in lovely, hilly surroundings. The last part of our journey was cross-country, some of the time riding alongside a beautiful and fairly wide river. Having been told that my companions all knew the way, I began to worry a bit when they kept stopping local peasants to ask directions. I was even less happy when they disagreed among themselves as to the correct route.

Although I like both Uras, they are hopelessly irresponsible and lose no opportunity of showing off their skills. Those skills are fairly childish. I did not have the heart to point out that we gave up going 'round the world' (both legs on the left side of the saddle, then astride facing the tail, then both legs on the right side of the saddle before returning to the normal position), lying along the horse's back, etc. when we were about nine years old. Mind you, they stole some lovely cucumbers and apples. Ura Kabil is to stay with us today and return tomorrow (I don't know how – with a bit of luck Anna and Peter will also go and take him with them). He gave me a crucifix for luck on the journey, which he told me that his mother had given to him.

28 July – DAY 2
Am boiling with rage. After endless faffing I finally managed to set off with Ura Kabil soon after 11am. We went cross-country all the way, along lovely tracks, over the hills and alongside some picturesque woods. In a funny way it can be quite depressing in this huge country – you breast a rise and can then see for about fifty miles, but know it will take more than a day to get to the next horizon.

I rode Rada, and Ura rode Masha, the black mare, with Pompeii tied to the back of Masha's saddle, leaving the grey (Malishka) to run free, and she never left our side. I was told we needed to cover fifty kilometres, but not told in which direction, nor that there were no plans for a rest (or lunch for us).

Ura Vadianov took over later. As we rode beside a huge wood we collected yet another cloud of gadflies. As usual they attacked Pompeii's private parts, and, in desperation, he suddenly stopped and rolled. Neither Masha nor Ura noticed in time, so we ended up with a broken bridle. After a while Ura started veering off in the wrong direction. I said nothing at first, assuming he knew this area well, but eventually could not refrain from pointing out that we had done almost a full circle and were now going east-north-east instead of west. He would not have it, but eventually I was proved right when Peter, Anna and Ura Kabil came panting up in the car yelling that we were going the wrong way. The situation was not improved by a violent thunderstorm.

By the time that was sorted and Ura Kabil and I rode in camp, we had done about sixty-five kilometres, fifteen of them quite unnecessarily. One episode really surprised me – we had been told to head for a particular village and checked with a local to see if we were heading along the right track. But the woman had no idea where that village was – it turned out to be about nine kilometres away! How can anyone never have heard of a village just over five miles distant?

Poor Masha was exhausted (she is probably the best horse, but she is the only one to have had to carry men virtually all day on both days – virtually because about an hour and a half before we got to camp I persuaded Ura Kabil to let me (50kg) ride her, instead of him (80+kg).

On the plus side we saw signs of wild boar.

We had supper, and I kissed goodbye to Anna, Peter and both Uras, and am now exhausted. I am quite proud of myself. I am the only one to have ridden all of both days, and the Cossacks are complaining about their arses and leg muscles.

29 July – DAY 3
Up at 7.30am, forgot it was my birthday till the men reminded me. It was so sweet, Lev gave me a bunch of dandelions and a packet of fags, and Vassily gave me a box of matches to go with it. We had to have a shot of vodka – surely the earliest I have ever had booze.

Off at 9am, with me on Pompeii leading Masha, Lev on Malishka leading Rada. We got on well at first, riding along pretty tracks across country, but soon we got lost and had to get across a gully with sheer sides. After studying the terrain for a while we found a place where, with some difficulty and not much danger, we were able to lead the horses down and up the other side. We then had to go through a field of sunflowers, which are very heavy and painful to hit! We went towards a farm to ask the way, but luckily we were seen from the road by Arman and Vassily and we were able to change the route slightly.

Soon after that we were followed by a car and a man got out and came towards me saying, 'Are you Barbara?'. I never found out how he knew my name, but he wanted to tell us that we had to be on our guard against gypsies who would surely steal our horses. I immediately saw every site as a gypsy one, but how would one tell? Apart from the fact that most people in this area are blond, any house or farm could be a gypsy camp at first sight.

Some peasants advised us of a short cut to the next meeting place and one went so far as to get his horse and show us the way. With he and Lev chatting away nineteen to the dozen we continued across country. The terrain here continues to be very attractive: slightly hilly, and with huge areas of meadowland. It is remarkable that there are so many woods and small copses. By some miracle we met up with the van and I insisted on a two-hour rest for the horses, who are still tired. It was then agreed we would do just another five or six kilometres before making camp. We think that while our maps of the area are such a ridiculous scale (1:2,500,000 or even 1:3,000,000), it would be better in future to follow the road so we don't lose each other again.

Later

Am spitting mad! Not only did the five or six kilometres turn into about twelve or fifteen (total for the day about forty- five), but the campsite I had understood to have been selected had not. Lev and I arrived at the place indicated (close to the road at the top of the hill, but well hidden behind a thick line of trees) to find no sign of the van. We sent up a flare and they found us, but now I don't trust them to stay awake and keep watch overnight. Instead of making camp at 7pm, yet again it was gone 9pm by the time we had settled the horses. We have tied them up in the trees with their feed and some stolen sweetcorn and shall tether them out in the open once it is dark enough. As I write I am looking over the lip of the hill, which drops quite dramatically to a small stream. Earlier on we saw a farmer on the other side herding about forty cows back to an invisible village. Unfortunately that probably means he saw us.

Once we have moved the horses, I am going to say a few words about how the horses are tired, thanks to Peter and Anna (and of course Ura who went the wrong way and cost us fifteen kilometres), and when I say five or six kilometres that is exactly what I mean.

30 July – DAY 4
6am

Well, last night we had a mutiny. They all feel there are not enough of us to guard and defend the horses because if Lev and I ride all day we can't take turns at staying awake at night. I said that if we stick to the roads so that Arman and Vassily could simply drive the agreed distance for the day, shopping if necessary on the way, they could then rest and thus be able to stand guard at night. I also suggested buying a can of paint so the drivers could leave signs for the riders. Lev thought we were at risk riding where we could be seen from the road and should ride across country, and that we ought to have four riders.

It was finally agreed that we should contact the local police and ask them:

1. Can they guard us?
2. Can they find a local vet for Malishka? (Lev says she is not moving properly, although I can't find anything wrong with her.)
3. Can they provide decent maps of this area and maybe the next?

I decided to sleep outside in a spare and smelly sleeping bag, and to set my alarm for 3.30am. When I checked the horses, nobody was awake. Woke again two hours later then dozed amid the insects until 5.45am, by which time Lev and Arman were awake. Lev then moved the horses back into the trees, Arman and I gave them oats, and Lev went back to sleep.

I am concerned about tethering the horses overnight. Malishka has got tangled up and panicked about five times, Masha only once, but that's bad enough. I am pleased with Pompeii – he is very quiet and sensible on the whole, and less nervous of people.

Both greys seem good horses, although I don't know what's wrong with Malishka.

Rada has the most energy so far, but kicks and bites both humans and horses. She doesn't like the others and Pompeii hates her, and she has been given far too much independence by Peter and has very much a mind of her own. She was found with a dreadful open wound on her shoulder the night before we left, which ought to have been stitched, but the Cossacks disagreed and I am putting antibiotic lotion on daily. All the horses are terribly scarred, especially when one considers that Pompeii, the eldest, is only five.

Until last night I slept in my own tent, on the (true) grounds that I sleep naked. I have brought a towelling robe which is very practical. I can put it on when I get up, which makes going to the loo much easier than when wearing trousers, and I can wash myself all over quite modestly. I think I am confirming everyone's idea of the eccentric English. I did try to buy a hammock while in Moscow, but I think this system is much better.

One extremely pleasant aspect of this situation is the joy of waking to the sound of horses grazing.

9:20pm
We set off around 9:45am and simply rode alongside the road for about two or three hours (including through a village). We could then see the town of Butulinovka.

Unfortunately, it being Rada's turn to be ridden by Lev today, she cannot lead another horse as she will kick it. This meant that riding Masha, I had to lead both Pompeii and Malishka. Lev said it was too dangerous but, as I pointed out, we had no choice. Actually on the whole it was fine until Masha thought the stream I was offering her to drink from was a puddle – the two led horses went eagerly to drink while she panicked and shot backwards. We sorted ourselves out in the end, with absolutely no help from Lev on the grounds that he could not bring Rada near the others. I'm sure he is sulking.

We stopped, tethered the horses and left them in the care of Lev and Vassily while I went with Arman to find the police station. We didn't, but we found a GAI (traffic police) station at the other side of town. When Arman explained our situation they said there were no gypsies around here. Young, unhealthy-looking louts swaggered about with their little Kalashnikovs, slouching and smoking on duty – they clearly thought it beneath their dignity to look surprised at our far-off destination. They drew a plan for Arman showing how we could get around the town off the asphalt.

I was really enjoying myself – not getting lost across country, even feeling slightly in control. The horses seem to have recovered. My companions, by contrast, have been doom and gloom all day – Lev hardly opened his mouth while we rode. He and I took the long, mainly dirt-track, route around the town, and after a couple of hours it became clear he did not know where to go. I had heard Arman shout to Lev as we parted 'If all else fails, we'll meet at GAI' so when Lev got lost I took us down there. We waited for forty minutes, whereupon Arman and Vassily turned up all hot and bothered, having been driving around town for hours, – God knows why – and looking for us.

Riding conditions have been dreadful. It was incredibly hot and dreadfully dusty as we rode round the town, and our route included going round a quarry and up a very steep hill which really made the horses puff.

I finally blew up when I realized Arman had not found anywhere to camp. Why not? He claimed he had not had time. Nonsense, I told him, he could have been looking for a camp-site instead of wasting petrol going all over town looking for us. His excuse was that we needed protection. He also stated that there were 'too many people living round here' and that it would get harder and harder to find camp-sites. While looking for a site the van became bogged down in mud, but we have finally found a lovely orchard. I have set my alarm to check the horses during the night.

After starting to type this, I had to stop for supper (packet soup, not much when you have had nothing to eat all day), and immediately after I learned one or two things that have really enraged me. The Russians complain that we are going too slowly, Nikolai Bezbatka had told them we could do 120km a day. I said that was rubbish, and that the best we could hope for was eighty kilometres a day when I had got the horses really fit. Now I am satisfied they are not exhausted we can go faster and further. 'Not possible,' said Arman. It turns out that Lev has not ridden for ten years and his bottom hurts.

I did not mince my words. The horses were not as fit as I had asked (and paid heavily) for them to be, they were ridden too far for the first two days, and if Lev had not ridden for ten years why the hell didn't he get fit first? Finally, if Anna and Nikolai thought we had enough people, what were they worrying about? (Arman tried to ring Anna today to say we need more people.) I told him quite clearly I am as anxious to hurry up as he is, but none of the stated reasons are my fault – so he need not look daggers at me.

It is now 10:15pm and I have just given the horses their oats, my so-called helpers having forgotten. I found Pompeii had wrapped his tether round a tree and was stuck. It is just as well I am checking in the night.

A final thought: there is nothing wrong with Malishka, Lev was just using her as an excuse for not pushing on faster.

31 July – DAY 5

I am now very tired. I was unable to get back to sleep after my 3.30am check, so I sat and pondered. I decided to send Lev back with Rada and continue, alone if necessary, but to see if Sasha [Morev] in Moscow could find someone else to ride with me. I know this is unkind to Lev, but I have to be ruthless if I am to succeed in this expedition. One thing I have had to learn – and quickly – is to be really assertive. I wonder what my family and friends will make of it, or if I will revert to the old me as soon as I get home. Getting these Russians moving is a nightmare, although I have to admit they wake up readily enough. Left to themselves they would spend literally three hours drinking tea, eating, smoking and chatting.

A good day. I roused everyone at 5.45am and we were on the move by 7.40am. There was lots of moaning about the fog and how dangerous it was to ride on verges that were ten yards wide, when anyone over three years old would have known it was the early morning promise of a hot day.

We plodded along the roadside, inching our way across the map at a snail's pace. We took a long lunch-break during which Arman and I went to phone Anna. We got through eventually, and she was predictably bossy and dictatorial. I shall ring her again tomorrow to tell her she has done enough harm. No luck getting through to Sasha. Lev spoke to Anna later, and somehow now seems happier – he will stay for two or three days. She said I must take Rada because my Customs document shows that I have four horses. I have decided to 'sell' Rada to Lev so as to be able to show why I only have three horses and I have told Arman that he must find a lawyer today so that we have a proper document for the document-loving Russian authorities.

Vassily told me that Lev had been given to understand that there would be three riders, with the Russians sharing the riding, whereas Anna wanted there to be three people riding at all times. Apparently Lev also thought there would a second back-up car, something that was never even thought of, let alone discussed as a serious possibility. Vassily does not like Anna. It is obvious that all the Russians on this trip thought it would be some kind of picnic.

Only about fifty kilometres today – I would have liked to have done as many miles.

We met a hobbled horse in a village and Pompeii reared up to defend his mares, with me on his back. It was more interesting than dangerous. We then met a loose unhobbled horse at the very end of the day, who was a frightful nuisance until Lev spent a quarter of an hour chasing it off with a stick. Still riding Pompeii, I retreated quietly out of sight. There was no doubt it was the stallion that the unhobbled horse was interested in.

Today I had to bandage Malishka, who has serious cuts to her off-side heel from getting tangled in her tether. There was much shrieking from Lev that I would get kicked, and it took me a while to persuade him to let me do it my way. With a continuous barrage of Russian mutterings of 'be careful', 'don't get kicked', 'mind your head' and so on, I eventually managed to make Malishka understand I was trying to help and succeeded in getting the bandage on. The only thing she managed to kick (I held on to her leg until she settled) was the lighter hanging round my neck. I have decided not to tether her any more, as she never seems to stray more than a few feet from Masha, and I must take the risk, or one morning we'll find she has cut her foot off.

We have ridden through several villages, and I noticed that thyme grows wild in the verges, where assorted livestock is staked out. This causes problems when Pompeii talks (or rather shouts) at the creatures, just like Aysha, my beloved old grey Arab mare back at home.

The people round here are reasonably friendly, and often shout to Lev asking if we are selling the horses, presumably because we have two spare ones. I am, of course, as a woman, completely ignored.

1 August – DAY 6
6am
A really beautiful morning. Arman photographed me using the Psion but unfortunately the camera battery is running out. Needless to say it is the only kind of which I have no spare, so I have asked Arman to see if by a miracle he can find a camera or battery shop in Liski today, while he is looking for a lawyer.

Arman must also get oats as we have nearly finished our supply. I am worried that all the horses are too thin, and think the quality of grazing is poor. They seem well, but no amount of oats will fatten them up, so I have also asked Arman to see if he can find some hay for tonight. Last night we stole sweetcorn cobs for them, which they love. On Lev's advice we left the outer leaves on, but removed the hairy parts.

I shall have to ride and lead two again today. This is tiring, partly because it is quite dangerous, and partly because we have to look extra hard at the ground knowing that, whichever for- mation we use (one led horse beside, one trailing behind or both led horses trailing behind) less than two abreast is not possible. There is so much to watch out for – rusty old iron and discarded farm or garden implements lying on the ground, not to mention occasional huge holes, empty vodka bottles, and the tether leads of innumerable goats and cows in the villages.

9pm
A much better day than anticipated. Riding up the main road towards Voronezh was excellent. All the horses were in fine fettle, to the extent that I could hardly restrain my three! Eventually I told Lev that I had to let them have a trot and that I would wait somewhere for him. I wonder if it is the vitamins I am gradually introducing, the horses having rejected the funny- smelling powder at first?

We must have done well over 50km today. I realized at lunch, after two brief trots, that my saddle sores and stiff knees have been made far worse by only proceeding at a walk. I now really can't wait to get rid of Lev. I have decided to take the day off tomorrow and go into Liski, the nearest town. I need to find a lawyer to draw up a contract with Lev, to phone Giles to see if he can get a rider from England, and to phone Anna to tell her straight that nobody provided by her has been of any use, so I don't want any more of them. We must also order a lorry to take Rada back, and find food for the horses.

One interesting event occurred today which confirms my feeling that the Russians are all incredibly honest. Against Lev's advice I stopped at a roadside kiosk to buy some mineral water. I asked the old woman within how much it cost, and she said six thousand roubles, so I paid her and she opened a bottle for me. Half an hour later (or more) as we turned off the main road, a man in a car drew up in front of me and stepped out. I was amazed when he gave me some money – apparently I had been charged for the wrong kind of water and this was my change. I could barely believe it – apart from anything else, the amount I paid was less than £1 so the change cannot possibly have been worth chasing me for.

There was an annoying, but revealing incident this morning. After setting out we returned to the river to water the horses. Lev waded in at the easiest place with Rada, thereby making it impossible for me to approach. I had to find somewhere else with my three, which is not easy when the one you are riding has to be persuaded that every drop of water is not a terrifying puddle.

The gadfly situation was terrible at lunchtime, and Vassily kindly took over my job of sweeping Pompeii's private parts with a branch, which at least prevents most of them settling. This evening he told me we should have taken a photo so he could return to his job as a mechanic and show his friends that he had acquired another skill. I said, 'That will be useful in Moscow', which they all thought hilarious. It produced the only smile all day from both Lev and Arman.

For once Arman has found a really good campsite with lots of really good grass surrounded by trees. Today we could be in a different country – the landscape has changed from undulating hills to much steeper ones, the soil here is very sandy, and the trees here are all conifers of one kind or another.

Lev has a strange way of speaking which he no longer bothers to adapt, so I can't begin to understand the few words he does bother to address to me.

One result of our snail's pace is that I have no time to relax and read. By the time I have fed the horses, taken down my tent, had breakfast, got the Russians moving and mounted up, ridden all day, looked for a campsite, unsaddled, tethered and fed the horses and then eaten, it has never been earlier than about 10pm. My alarm goes off at 2.30am when I check the horses, and again at 5.30am to get up. I am not as tired as I ought to be, but I am probably running on boiling rage.

In spite of all my moaning, however, I really am enjoying myself.

In Liski, at my insistence, we went to Customs, which we have just left (11am) – brilliant! I was assured there would be no problems at the border with only three horses, and the female Customs official was very friendly and helpful, suggesting we leave Rada at a local race-yard, where they have agreed to take her for about three months. It may be best to transport all the horses there and then back again although it is doubling back on our route. They have a farrier, which we urgently need. We also hope they have oats, the lack of which has become a very pressing problem.

Hope my luck lasts.

Booking a phone call to England can take up to twenty-four hours, so if we have no luck here I shall ask Arman to drive me to Voronezh where there are direct-dial international telephones, which is a real wonder.

I rang Anna, who is ordering impotently from Moscow that I must do this, I cannot do that, finishing with 'I have found somebody to ride with you, it is just a question of payment. . . .!' I simply said firmly, 'No, Anna'.

9pm
Well, after much messing around we have got some oats ('no payment required, we wish you luck on your journey') and the stud will take Rada for up to three months at a cost of US $250 (£165) per month. We are to call at 7am to guide their horsebox to the campsite and to collect all the horses. I don't think I'll be able to ride further than to a new camp site because I cannot guess how long it will take to load four semi-wild horses into a box and then shoe three of them. I just hope the shoes I brought from England fit – I selected the size from a fax of a tracing Anna made around one of the horse's feet, but when I got here and enquired whose foot she had thus traced, she said it was Malishka, whose hooves had been so overgrown they had to be trimmed by the Cossacks.

We drove ninety kilometres each way, to Voronezh, which lies on a very wide part of the Don, and is much less grim than most Soviet cities, to phone Giles. Although I tried for well over an hour, the international lines (line?) from Voronezh were engaged the whole time. I am desperate to speak to Giles, but shall have to try and ring Sasha tomorrow and ask him to fax Giles. Maybe I will ask Sasha if he knows someone who can ride with me until Giles can get someone from England.

I shall also ask Giles if he can pull strings with his Army friends and get a couple of soldiers out in a Landrover. I just don't trust this lot – after staring at the map for hours (and I shall do the itinerary in future) I can see that our current position is a complete dead-end. Arman does not drive well, can't select a campsite, panics if he can't find me for half an hour, does not shop for fresh food, and sulks at every opportunity. I am half expecting to wake up one morning to find myself alone. I do not think even a Muscovite can handle taking orders from a woman, although I have tried very hard not to be bossy but to say things like, 'Do you think you could find some water for the horses?' and 'Is there any chance of buying oats in the next village?'

Arman does have a point about the map. When Nikolai Bezbatka at the Academy of Sciences said they would provide the maps and the itinerary, I thought they would at least be decent maps. I knew that in the past maps were a state secret, but expected something better than a road atlas with a scale of 1:2,000,000 or 1:3,000,000. At least half of the roads are just not shown because they are too small to bother with. Arman was given no itinerary, will not listen to me, and seems to be just haphazardly zig-zagging across the map.

I am very tired today, probably because I have had no exercise. After a wet start to the day it has been boiling hot and I am still really hot and sticky in the van with a silent and sullen Arman, returning from the abortive trip to the telephone in Voronezh.

3 August – DAY 8
Arman asked me to wake him at 5.45am for a 6.15am start to the stud, the theory being (or so I thought) that if we were there at 7am we could guide the horsebox back to the camp, load all the horses, get the three remaining ones shod, leave Rada, and carry on. Hah! Arman was still shaving at 6.40am, so I tried to hurry

him, but when we got to the stud we found we had to ask the director if we could hire a lorry, but of course he was too busy to talk to us for nearly an hour. When I finally saw the lorry I refused it – our cattle would have looked askance at it and I don't want this lot ruined.

The farrier was also too busy to shoe the horses – he had to go and do a roofing job in Voronezh.

Back at the camp we tacked up and set off, with me riding Pompeii and leading two mares. Lev was ruder than ever, grunting and pointing left or right if he thought I was going the wrong way, and continually telling me on which side of the road to ride. I can't wait to get rid of him.

We stopped to give the horses a drink from a small river, but Pompeii went in too far and to my absolute horror we started sinking in the mud. I shouted and drove him on back to the bank as far as I could, then jumped off and pulled him and yelled encouragement, and after many heart-stopping seconds he got himself free. Far from being shaken by his experience, he started grazing almost before his hind-legs were out of the mud!

Today, yet again, it was sweltering hot and swarming with flies, but at least there were no gadflies. I am being good about sun cream, but the hairs on my forearms are white.

Malishka has been a perfect bloody nuisance today, pulling back so hard she almost dragged me out of the saddle several times. It only seems to happen when we are riding along on roads, so I think her feet must hurt. Unfortunately today most of our route was roadwork.

I have pulled a muscle in my groin (left side, so a particular nuisance when mounting up), but don't know how. Malishka trod on my foot (everyone made a frightful fuss when Pompeii did the same on Tuesday) and Masha bit me on the elbow, which I think was a mistake as I feel sure she didn't mean it. Apart from these assorted bruises, grazes and insect bites, I am fine, although I think I may have some trouble with a rope burn on my right palm from literally dragging Malishka along. I intend to ride her tomorrow, so it ought to be easier.

Arrived at the stud after a blazing row with Arman who wants me to take the small roads. I told him no, not until he had found a farrier and the horses were shod, my experience so far being the bigger the road, the wider the verge. I also told him to stop treating me as a bloody nuisance. Then I was told the van had broken down – something electric – so we have stabled my other three horses here with Rada for one night. I expected something better, but no – they are tied up in filthy stalls with no bedding. At least it is no worse than what they are used to.

I now hate Arman like poison. He (like Lev) never smiles, never speaks to me unless he has to, never offers help, never tells me what is going on, and sulks as if all these disappointments and delays are my fault.

I am desperate to get to a phone and ask Giles to send me some help. Apart from general incompetence (even regarding little things such as half the equipment in the van is chucked in a different place every morning, so I can never find anything), this breakdown of the van worries me – it probably won't be the last, and guess who has to pay?

Vassily, the only decent chap, is worried that I am not eating enough. He is kind, offers help, talks to me – a miracle of manners in this company.

Later
After seemingly endless head-scratching and orders and counter-orders, Vassily (who has done less than anyone but who told me he is a mechanic) has just informed me that we need to buy a new generator tomorrow at a cost of 200,000-300,000 roubles (around £35) which sounds pretty reasonable.

For some reason the atmosphere today has been much lighter and friendlier than usual, to the extent that Lev even offered to help me put up my tent. It's his last night, which may explain his kindness.

4 August – DAY 9
I slept badly last night and woke exhausted. Usually I lie down thinking that I'll never sleep because the ground is so hard and the next thing I hear is the alarm. There was no reason for it. The horses were in the stables, so I didn't have to check them at 2.30am, and I had put my tent under some birch trees, so instead of a soggy, dew-ridden tent it was bone dry.

We went to the stud, and found the horse happily eating hay but on the ground was a foetus – one of the mares had miscarried. Since I had given instructions that they were not to be covered, I was very surprised. It was probably Malishka (she was the closest to it) which might explain her intransigence yesterday, and Arman told me that she 'had something hanging out the back', which I should have been told at the time.

I set off with Valery who is the stud's chief horseman, who was to show me a short-cut. He fancies himself no end – he has long, curly, very carefully-arranged blond hair, and kept slipping his jacket off so I could admire his torso. We had a lovely ride through woods and across meadows, and then we had to get off to go under a railway line. The tunnel was only just high enough for the unmounted horses, although I half expected Masha's saddle to be scraped off – at well over sixteen hands she is the biggest horse.

When we rejoined the road at the appointed place there was no sign of my team for half an hour (surprise, surprise). Then we had to ride along asphalt roads, (which is becoming increasingly painful for the horses, but the only farrier we could find was drunk), before stopping for a rest. I blew my top when I was told we had to turn south again because there were no bridges across the Don. They all shouted at me that it was not their fault. I agree the maps are lousy, but I still think Arman has brought us to the wrong area in the first place.

I spoke quietly to Arman later, saying that if I had been involved or consulted at any stage then it would have been a joint decision and I wouldn't have flown off the handle. I also said that we were stuck with each other for a few weeks so we might as well try to be friends. He went even sulkier and refused to translate what I had said although Vassily wanted to know. Since then, however, he and Lev have been much nicer and Lev has again helped me with my tent. I have told Anna that if Lev wants to hang around a bit longer that's fine – he has been much more helpful since he stopped riding. Arman took me to a nearby village to phone Sasha, and I managed to speak to him at last and he will try to find another rider. I am to ring him again tomorrow at 8am before he goes to his *dacha*. I also asked Sasha to ring Giles and let him know I am alive and well. I was unable to say anything more as there is no privacy in that post office, and my relationship with Arman is strained enough already. I shall ask him to drive me to Voronezh when we get a bit closer, which may even be tomorrow night if the horses get a move on.

We did about fifty kilometres today, but this is quite meaningless as we are now going south again. We are about eight or nine kilometres from the Don, after crossing which I plan to strike off across country to cut the corner and avoid a fair-sized town. I shall then pick up the smaller Voronezh road where I ought to make fairly good time. The mares are going well, especially Maliskha (surprising after her miscarriage), but lazy old Pompeii is still lagging behind. I shall ride Malishka tomorrow for the first time.

Our campsite tonight is about one and a half kilometres from the road, again well hidden behind a wood. Whatever else, as long as we are in Russia I can't see that we will ever be forced to camp where we can be seen by the passing traffic.

5 August – DAY 10

We were bombarded by a terrific thunderstorm in the early hours, and when we got up we found wolf footprints near the horses. On the way to the post office to phone Sasha the van became stuck in the mud and then would not go into reverse gear, so I had to walk over a mile back to camp to get the others to help.

As we were tacking up, Lev found a mouse in my saddle.

Malishka is a bit headstrong but very comfortable. Thirty minutes after we set off we were caught in a major thunderstorm – I had taken my jacket and hat at the last minute but not the waterproof trousers. The waxed cotton hat that I bought in Newmarket turns out not to be waterproof.

We came to the famous River Don to find that the only bridge for miles in any direction was a floating, rusty iron one, full of holes. The horses were understandably not too keen, and we had to wait while a bride was carried across, which is obviously a local custom, as another bride suffered the same fate half an hour later. I decided to go first, leading Pompeii – he is the oldest, and I wasn't about to forget that the two mares were so wild when I saw them in February that they had to be trussed up like chickens to be looked at. He was very brave and trusting, and the mares followed like lambs.

Safely on the other side we then had hours of talk with some locals about the next stage of our journey. I wanted to cut across country, but was told by Arman after repeatedly requesting to know what was being said that there might be 'problems'. When I asked what kind of problems, he ignored me and walked off, as usual.

Eventually it was revealed that there was a farrier in the village – he seemed sober and I liked the look of him. Since the horses' feet obviously hurt them on tarmac, where it is frequently necessary to go and since their hooves were wearing down at an alarming rate, it was agreed they should be shod for US $20 (£13) per horse, which was a figure I came up with as nobody knew what the going rate was.

The horses were duly led to the smithy – a little open-sided shed with a roof, and just big enough to accommodate one horse, with a breast-bar at the front and another at the back. To my horror, whichever leg was being shod was tied up. Considering they have never even had their feet picked out before, I thought they were all very good, especially Masha who was done first. Both Malishka and Pompeii gave me a few nasty moments when they (understandably) panicked. Malishka was the worst, and, rather belatedly, they finally decided to rope in the sides to keep her straight.

The actual shoeing was fascinating. The hooves were trimmed to fit the shoe, rather than the opposite, and in Russia they trim off the frog. I should have thought that must be very painful as well as making the horses clumsier. [The frog is a frog-shaped pad located in the middle of the underside of the hoof, and is the only part of the horse's foot which is sensitive.]

There were four men helping the farrier, not counting our crew. I offered to help, but of course my offer was ignored – they may be my horses, it may be my expedition, I may be the one paying, but I am only a woman.

This episode has confirmed my suspicions that the Russians are actually afraid of horses. Why else would they insist on tying up the leg being shod? Why else was Lev so horrified at my determination to bandage Malishka's off-hind leg?

About five hours after crossing the Don we were ready to go, except that in all the excitement of being shod Malishka suddenly came into season. Since I was riding alone and could never have coped, we did the only thing possible and let Pompeii mount her. We continued quietly for just over an hour, whereupon she broke her bridle and I dismounted, bowed to the inevitable and let Pompeii mount again. This was right beside the road, and a passing motorcyclist almost fell off with surprise.

We found a reasonable campsite but with very little grass, and almost immediately Vassily started telling me that it was getting harder and harder to find grazing, and would continue to get harder. I told him it was not my fault, that Anna had said that it would be easy until we got to the West where we could buy hay.

I am very worried about food. Oats seem hard to come by, and we can't always steal corncobs, goose grass or, (in desperation tonight), straw.

As I was very publicly a foreigner with dollars in the village tonight and after last night's wolf prints, (quite apart from Malishka being in season – she has been put down wind of the stallion), I have told Arman we must keep watch tonight and that tomorrow I will get up at 4am to feed the horses, and that we must leave at 5am. The buckets of oats have been set ready, as has some water for me to wash, so I shan't have to wake Vassily, who sleeps in the van.

These blokes continue to behave as if it were their expedition into which I have rudely intruded with my horses. They nag daily that I should hire a lorry and just load up the horses – and they are quite serious.

Ladybirds all along this ride have been ten a penny, and we have seen thousands of lizards, toads and grasshoppers. There are also millions of hares, but no rabbits in this part of Russia, (so rabbit holes are not a danger), and I have yet to see a pheasant. Tonight when we arrived at camp we disturbed a large bird which I asked Arman to film: I think it may have been a kite or a small eagle. Considering the great outdoors is our lavatory, I am delighted to find that so far we have not encountered any stinging nettles.

6 August – DAY 11
We had to let Pompeii mount Malishka last night. This morning when I got up at 4am and fed them he seemed quiet enough, but she had managed to escape from her bridle. Since the Russians seldom have headcollars, and I had foolishly not brought any with me, we simply take the bits out of the horses' mouths in the evening, and so their bridles function as such.

Pompeii had her once more at 5.15am and showed no interest thereafter. We covered about sixty to sixty-five kilometres, and are now in a very poor area with no grazing, and it seems nobody has any hay for sale. The soil here is still very sandy, which may explain the lack of decent grass.

I took a short cut through a village and everyone panicked because they lost me for ten minutes.

I am exhausted now. Arman and I went off in the van in a vain attempt to find hay. I then asked him to drive me to Voronezh to telephone Giles, but he refused on the grounds that the van might break down. I did try to ring Sasha from the local post office, but it was closed. That is quite surprising, as post offices in Russia seem to function for very long hours, which I suppose is perfectly practical if the staff are paid only a pittance. Indeed, in big towns the post office is open around the clock.

7 August – DAY 12

I had a talk with Arman yesterday during our lunch break. He is, as is Vassily, deeply worried about the horse food situation – they assure me the regions we are going to go through are even poorer than this one.

'Then we must overcome the problem', I said, pointing out that my experience of Russian officials (Sergei Chulkov, the administrator in Alexikovo, and the Customs woman in Liski) is that they can be helpful. I asked Arman to go to the next biggish town (or to Kursk if necessary), explain our predicament and ask for help. What really maddens me is the attitude of helplessness. Talk about not a shred of initiative. . . .

Then I suggested buying a trailer so we can go to wherever necessary and buy enough oats and hay to last a week. 'We don't have a trailer bar,' cried Arman. I suggested gently, 'Well, see if you can find someone to put one on. Why did we not bring a roof rack, as we were supposed to?' Again, his only response was a shrug of helplessness.

I could scream, and meanwhile the horses are hungry.

7pm

I found some excellent grazing beside the road this morning, and gave the horses forty-five minutes of munching time. I was riding Masha, so did not have to dismount when Pompeii became randy and got his leg(s) over Malishka in the middle of a small village, to the outrage of two old women who opened the door of their cottage to see what the fuss was.

The horses then had four hours' grazing, while Arman and I went to Stari Oskol and I actually got through to Giles, who was amazed. I failed to get through to Sasha, though, as the operator said there was no answer from his office – tosh! From previous experience, I know that Sasha's office number is constantly engaged, so obviously the operator could not be bothered to keep trying. Stari Oskol must be the most hideous town I have ever seen – Stalinist concrete blocks of flats dominate the skyline in every direction.

The afternoon started well, as I found a lovely ride through a wood, which lasted a mile or so. The rest of the ride was a nightmare, along a road with very little verge, and through villages thereby attracting a lot of attention. I have told Arman he must let me go across country, especially tomorrow when he planned to make me ride up the main road to Stari Oskol, which has no verges. I told him I was much more likely to be killed there than in the countryside.

Arman and I also discussed the flare situation. Although several have been let off since we left Alexikovo, only one has actually fulfilled its purpose and been seen by the other party. I suggested to Arman that we should have a fixed time, say 7pm, when he should fire a flare if he couldn't find me. I am reluctant to set any off myself as, understandably, the horses are frightened by the swish of the rocket, so I would have to dismount, tie all three up and walk at least a hundred yards away.

I am desperately tired, so hope to unpack the van now, then go and try Sasha again. The Russians are still wallowing in gloom and doom and helplessness: it is slowly driving me mad. I hope I have the strength to refrain from strangling Arman one day.

Weather yesterday and today was cool and showery, which was not much fun for me, but much nicer for the horses.

10.30pm

I finally got through to Sasha. He has not found a rider yet but Anna Shubkina told him she had two riders available. I had to explain to Sasha why I did not want them. I just may recant, however, because I can tell Anna she can pay the new rider and get the money back from Lev. Giles will do what he can from England and I shall ring Sasha again tomorrow night after 9pm. What a good and useful man he is.

Lev is still here, although he was supposed to go today. Vassily is angry, apparently with me – why? – and reiterated for about the ninth time he just wants to go home.

8 August – DAY 13

Up at 5am to move the horses out of the field of oats which we put them in after dark last night. Back to sleep until nearly 8am.

A truly glorious morning, and by getting up late I had the luxury of washing in warm water. These Russians never seem to wash, and hardly ever change their clothes, although I have found one or the other cleaning his teeth occasionally.

Over breakfast, another blow. Vassily wants to go home now. He is afraid of bandits (he thinks our party is too small) and does not want to be used as a driver. Every day he has warned me of the dangers of bandits, and is convinced we will wake up one morning with our throats cut. I told Arman it was up to the Institute to provide another groom until Giles can organize one from England, and that I hoped Vassily would stay until a replacement had been found. I also said that, if Sasha could not find another rider, I would (to make Arman happy), have a rider provided by Anna, again until Giles has found one.

I said that (to put it crudely) I had paid Lev to come to England but, if he would come as far as Poland, he could keep the money, otherwise I would have to ask for most of it back. I did not hear that being translated.

I repeated how disappointed I had been that the people found by Anna had let me down, but that I had been planning this trip for a year and there was no way I was going to give up, even if it meant buying a cart and continuing alone. This would have been quite practical, because I could have kept the oats, tents etc. in the cart, and the horses could have taken it in turns to pull it, with the other two tied to the back of it. The only problem would be that I don't think my command of the Russian language is good enough to cope entirely by myself, and I sleep so deeply I might not hear it if wolves attacked the horses in the night.

Arman is hoping the new driver and rider will come by car as he thinks a second one is necessary. At what cost, one wonders?

I set off late (10am) thanks to all this and had no difficulty with following tracks through the woods. The great joy with these horses, so far from home and so much of a group, is that if you drop the lead of one of them it does not matter as they either stand there eating or follow on, as if still being led.

I had not eaten enough, and, as a result, got a bad headache, so I asked Arman for some bread and cheese. It turned out we were right by a *Stalovia* (a workman's café) so we went in turns to eat there. The café itself was a very grotty 1950s canteen and the food was plain and seemed quite wholesome. In the corner was a rare sight for us – basins with taps with running water.

One old man (NB don't listen to old men) said there was a track running north-north-west all the way to Kaplina. There was one, for a while, which led me into a field of potatoes and then vanished. After some thought, I rode across the field, crossed a road and set off across another huge field where they were combining. Half-way across, I thought I saw the van two or three miles away (eastwards) crawling along a *passadka*. Hell, I must be too far west, I thought – and I had wondered why I had not seen them before.

We returned to the road and trotted up it – God, the Russians come terrifyingly fast and close to the horses – but there was no sign of the van, so I waited by the road. It was just on 7pm, so I scanned the skies all around for a flare, but there was nothing. Eventually they came panting up, crying that they had been looking for me for three hours (not true, I had left them less than three hours previously). I explained what had happened, showed Arman the field from which I thought I had seen them, and he confirmed I had been right. I could not resist saying that it was a mystery, in that case, that they had lost me. It proves my point – they are hopeless at finding me.

9:30pm
The Russians have been sitting and talking, making no move to do anything. I can't phone Sasha as promised because Arman is afraid to drive down this little road in the dark – *honestly*. There is still no sign of any food, although they found me over two hours ago – no, wrong, they have just called me to eat. Unfortunately, there is no water to wash my hands, only enough for their precious tea. When I asked, Arman crossly informed me that there had been 'no time to get any because we were looking for you.'

9 August – DAY 14
Up at 6am to feed horses: my eyes are terribly swollen and sore, especially the left one, and I think I must have been stung in the night. Found the first stinging nettles of the ride the hard way, when going to the loo! I am no botanist, but have noticed lots of

tansy and what I think is cinque- feuille and tarragon. Trees seem just like at home, apart from lots of pines in sandy areas – oak, beech, rowan, sycamore and the inevitable birch.

Apart from around gardens, the only other fences I have seen so far are around cemeteries, which seemed odd at first sight, but of course the purpose is to keep assorted animals out, not to confine the dead. These cemeteries are usually a mile or so from the villages and never seem to have any connection with churches. The latter are few and far between and all in a dreadful state of neglect and decay.

My right knee has become very painful on dismounting, but I have learned that if I take my feet out of the stirrups every half-hour or so that helps ease the stiffness. The pain is probably referred from my back – the horses being led can be very obstinate and sometimes they literally have to be dragged. I have given up tying them to the saddle, as it is bad for the ridden horse and often results in broken bridles. It is better to drop the lead if there are problems.

All the tack is disgracefully badly made. I have only two vaguely usable bridles out of four, and have ripped two pairs of trousers on bits of metal sticking out of my saddle. I must ask Giles if he can possibly send two saddles, two bridles and some proper head-collars.

8am

I am at the post office in Stari Oskol waiting for the call to Giles which I booked ten minutes ago and watching the girl at the counter. The customer writes down the town, phone number and how many minutes are required. The girl then fills in a form, tears off the top piece (using a ruler, nothing as sophisticated as perforations) and gives it to the customer. The other piece is glued to the original paper. When the call is completed, a computer(!) print-out appears, and each set of papers gets 'filed' with the others by pushing a piece of wire through it, there is no hole punch. All calls and costs are logged on a form that the girl has to draw herself, using a carbon copy. When I was here the other evening it took ten minutes for the cashiers to hand over control.

It seems even at this level that the Russian attitude to authority is just as their literature suggests. The people with any authority do not just enjoy their little bit of importance, they revel in it and lord it over anyone in a position of servitude – in this case the poor person trying to make a telephone call. These girls at the Post Office seldom smile and seem really to enjoy making the customers wait, but I suppose they, too, have to take their turn when customers and somebody else lords it over them.

Later
Just as I had given up hope, the call to Giles was connected! He is sending a Landrover with a soldier called Richard Adamson and my old friend, Alison Lea, loaded with HorseHage, oats and tack. [HorseHage is a specialist horse food which is marvellous dust-free hay. All horses love it and thrive on it, and they never get coughing problems with it.] I am to ring him in three days to see what progress has been made – but I have asked him to get them to hurry.

Arman rang Ura Prisheppa (the dreaded Anna's boss), who, it turns out, has gone to Vietnam so now nobody knows what to do. Arman is convinced we are to be attacked by bandits at every turn. Arman and Lev continue to be incredibly rude, while Vassily is getting less friendly as he perceives the danger increasing.

Coming back to the campsite, Arman took a wrong turn in the woods and the van became stuck (it has been pouring since about 7am). It now seems that the gear-box has gone (a simple piece of information which had to be prised from Arman), and they are working on it at the moment. I hope Vassily really is a mechanic.

It is quite clear that the van is completely useless, and – if I can ever get Arman to listen to me – I plan to get him to take me into Stari Oskol (we are camped on the edge of it at the moment). There I plan to find somebody in authority and find out if there are any stables in the area which can take the horses for a week or so, and then locate a hotel, preferably one with a telephone. Vassily and Arman (and maybe Lev?) can drive the van back to Moscow while I wait here, then Arman can take the train back and rejoin me once the Brits arrive.

I don't really care if I never see them again, but I must ring Sasha and ask him either to find me an English-speaking Russian co-driver or to ask Giles if he can possibly find a Russian speaker to come with the Landrover. Apart from actually asking the way, buying petrol, etc., they will need to be able to read the maps.

Later still
Well, they all loved my idea! Arman and I went and found a

helpful administrator and a local farmer (Nikolai Myelnikov) was found who would keep the horses for a week or two at a cost of US $10 (£6.60) per day per horse. I said I knew I was paying a lot but I wanted to be certain they would be safe. He is also storing all my equipment. He is fair, fat and (unusually for here) has mutton-chop whiskers.

I was pleased to discover that the centre of Stari Oskol is very old and beautiful: the river Oskol runs through it and lovely old buildings line the hilly streets. The word *Stari* means old, so maybe there is a *novi* (new) Oskol somewhere nearby.

While we were waiting (if nothing else, I have learned patience on this trip) the men discussed Vassily's favourite subject – bandits – with Oleg, a friend of Nikolai's. He told us it was quiet here, but that there were many bandits and it was very dangerous further on. I have heard this before and it reminds me of Robin Hanbury-Tenison's experience in South America, where the fiercest tribes were always several miles further on.

Eventually a friend of Nikolai's appeared, and he and I rode to the farm. It was supposed to be ten kilometres, but we trotted almost the whole way and it took over two hours, so it must have been much further. I am happy that the horses will be safe: there is a vicious Great Dane type (but black and bigger) by the gate, and a hulking Caucasian Arfchatka [an equally vicious sheepdog which is capable of seeing off a wolf] chained up by the back door. Also, the horses are in a paddock, not chained up as previously, which is a nice change for them.

Nikolai also showed us a proper Cossack saddle and bridle, which was magnificent. I hope Lev took note: he already knows how displeased I am with the tack I got from Peter.

The farm consists of a long, low cow shed, with the usual rubbish and rusting old bits and pieces in the yard. I was surprised to be offered food, but it turned out that the family (Nikolai, Tatiana and their two sons) live in one end of the cow shed. There is a very strange mixture of luxury and primitiveness, in that Tatiana has no running water in the house, but they have a phone from which you can call England, and a television and video machine with a remote control.

To my great delight, at the other end of the cow shed, past the cows and horses, was a Bannia, which is really just like a sauna, so I later sweated, scrubbed, washed my hair and felt really clean for the first time since leaving Moscow. Getting dressed was quite difficult as about 200 young chickens sleep in what should be the ante-room to the Bannia, and I did not want either to tread on one of them or, in my new, clean state, to step in any chicken-shit.

More food was then offered, and the men all used the Bannia. Oleg had earlier suggested that, instead of going to an hotel, I could stay with a friend of his in town, which would be much nicer and I would only have to pay half the cost of an hotel. I had agreed with delight – it would be much more fun and I would get a lot more practice in speaking Russian. Unfortunately, we talked for so long about horses that we suddenly realized it was far too late to go back to town this evening. Oleg went off with all my luggage and I slept here with the others. I was tired and went to bed just before midnight, but I think I slept in a dormitory with Vassily, Arman, Lev and the two sons. It was dark, so I was not sure how many beds there were – only that I did have one to myself.

CHAPTER FIVE

On a Russian Farm

10 August – DAY 15

Woke at 8am having slept like a log. Luckily I did not have to get up for a pee during the night, as getting past the dog is a nerve-wracking experience and would have woken everyone up.

I am getting tired of noting this, but Tatiana works non-stop and the men sit around doing nothing, although I notice the boys help her a bit. She makes everything herself – cheese, condensed milk, cream and something called chocolate butter that I have not had the courage to try. And she made huge mounds of pancakes for breakfast.

She and Nikolai sleep in the kitchen/living room, the bed being partly screened behind a curtain, which reminded me of the Mongolian gers I had grown accustomed to when riding round the High Altai mountains last summer. The room where I spent the night is the next shed and the only other room. There is a half-built house in the yard, so perhaps they are going to live in that? Tatiana at least must know there is a better life, as her mother lives in Germany and Tatiana has visited her there. Or can there still be Germans who live like this?

Living next to the animals (who are presumably never mucked out) means there are a zillion flies. I mean literally next to – on the other side of the wall behind my head the horses are living. Last night I noticed a small, white worm or maggot wriggling on the tablecloth, but I was so hungry I carried on eating and simply accepted an extra glass of vodka.

My team have now gone. I received a genuine kiss and hug from Vassily and a reluctant one from Lev and Arman – so here I am, alone among strangers, none of whom speaks a word of

English, in the middle of Russia. I found out later that my so-called supporters never even told Tatiana that they were going (let alone said 'thank you' or 'good bye'), so she cooked far too much lunch.

I was able to ring Giles, but it was a dreadful line. We talked for eight minutes (although the Russian operator said it was ten and charged us accordingly) at a cost of 8,400 roubles per minute (about US $1.80), and I explained to Giles exactly what was going on. He told me he had sent Anna a fax in which he described Arman as 'bad-tempered and useless'.

Talking to Tatiana, she made an interesting comment on the changes here. In the old days of Communism, they all had money but there was nothing in the shops to buy, and now they can buy almost anything but they don't have any money. She said that, on balance, most Russians preferred the older system. I said the changes were probably not so great for her, as she has cows for milk and meat, chickens for eggs and meat, a vegetable garden, etc., and she told me she hardly buys anything except sugar and salt. Most years she does not even need to buy flour, but apparently this year they had not grown enough wheat (or the crop was inadequate, due to the drought) – I am not sure which.

Oleg came to fetch me at lunch-time. All these people are horrified at the lack of preparation for this expedition – inadequate transport, no proper maps, no itinerary, nobody to advise me on which horses to buy (it seems the ones I have are not really native ones), the list goes on. Mind you, the Russians are quicker than most to point out where other people have gone wrong. They are all much amused at my frequent use of the Russian word meaning 'useless'.

Oleg said we ought to have a rifle with us on the trip as there are quite a lot of wolves about in the forests of the Bryansk region.

We went to where Oleg works – a shop selling French scents and cosmetics, where I met a wonderful woman called Zeena, and it is in her flat that I am staying. She is warm, vibrant, loud, large, with dark, curly hair, lots of make-up and the regulation gold teeth, dressed extremely colourfully, and I took to her at once. I was not surprised to find that she is a Leo and it is her birthday in about ten days' time.

She has two daughters, Lena and Svetlana, and they both seem very pleasant, and a husband, also Nikolai or Kol, who seems very kind, but is rather bullied by Zeena – he was only allowed one glass of vodka. I am still having difficulties with the local accent, but luckily both Zeena and Tatiana make an effort to tone it down and speak a little more slowly for my benefit. The daughters, too, make a special effort when talking to me. Like all Russian daughters I have met so far, they are incredibly dutiful, and are always helping their mother with whatever she requires.

I am fascinated by the friendship between these two women. Tatiana in her ill-fitting blue nylon dress, kerchief round her dark hair, a life of pure drudgery from one end of the day to the other (although I notice she is quite capable of joining in a conversation and actually seems very happy); and Zeena in her modern flat with hot and cold running water (she has told me with great pride that the water was hot all day), central heating, clothes, make-up and jewellery, and a job in a shop selling only luxuries.

11 August – DAY 16
Woke three times in the night with truly dreadful diarrhoea. Thank God that at the last moment I insisted on taking the medical kit with me, rather than leaving it at the farm. Thank God, too, that I am in this flat and not on the farm, as I doubt I would have made it to the privy in time.

I have decided to explain to Oleg the problem of finding a co-driver and ask him if he knows anyone who speaks English (although I doubt if he does or they would have been wheeled out for my benefit) and who would be prepared to go to the Polish–Belarussian border to guide my crew back here.

I washed my clothes, but some were so filthy from horses (and one pair of socks that got dunked – when Pompeii went swimming – and then stayed wet all day inside brown boots) that they are not at all clean, only no longer smelly. When Zeena got back from work she was horrified and insisted I wash them again with her washing powder.

In order to prevent her shovelling endless food inside me, I have had to confess to slight stomach-ache and slight diarrhoea. Actually, touch wood, the antibiotics are working. It is obviously not the done thing in Russia to still be thin at my age. Apparently there is a Russian saying, 'A woman without a bottom is like *Pyelmyeny* without meat'. [Pyelmyeny is a classic Russian dish, originally from Siberia, and is like ravioli.]

I learned something very interesting today. Before lunch I watched a Russian film that was set in the time of Tsar Alexander and discovered that the 'new' flag of Russia is the same as it was before the revolution.

The Russian women cook entirely by instinct – I don't believe any of them own scales, and I have only ever once seen anything measured at all, and that was when preserving tomatoes. Everything they do own is cheap and tacky, and I don't think it is just a case of affordability: I honestly think they simply don't care about anything or for anything except food. It is rare to see anything being cleaned except the work surface, and anything good or valuable (furniture, shoes, clothes) must just die of neglect and be wasted.

Kol brought me some flowers when he returned this evening – so sweet! He has taken rather a fancy to this exotic stranger in the family home, and keeps talking to me. Unfortunately he still does not think to soften his accent or slow his speech, so it is .a real struggle for me to keep up. He is always bare-chested, for which he apologized right at the beginning. I gathered he had some kind of accident (later revealed to be a scald from the pressure cooker).

12 August – DAY 17

There is something I keep forgetting to note. When the Russians complain about how little they earn, I sympathize, but I tell them that, in the West, there would only be one very busy person in an office which, in Russia, is staffed by three or four. That one person earns three or four times as much as each Russian, but the price we pay is very high unemployment. When I say this, they lose interest immediately. Are they supremely uninterested in how we do things, do they feel I am criticizing their comparative idleness, or do they simply switch off at the thought of a really hard day's work?

Everyone (Zeena, her family and Oleg) is off to Moscow, and I was invited to go too, but I told Zeena that after spending nearly two months waiting in the capital, I thought I would prefer to spend a few days on the farm with Nikolai and Tatiana.

I paid for my one-minute phone call to England, and asked rather diffidently whether I could pay for my keep so far, or if she would prefer me to settle up at the end. To my horror, Zeena point-blank refused to accept any payment, saying I was her guest. No, I said firmly, it had been agreed with Oleg that I would stay on the basis of paying her instead of an hotel. She told me to shut up. This certainly means I must go shopping and buy some treats.

It is obvious that these people here are a step up from the Alexikovo lot (although certainly no richer). They don't use the dreadful swear words that I have become accustomed to hearing, and I notice that everyone says 'thank you' when they leave the table. They also take the trouble to grow flowers and to cut flowers for the house and, amazingly, Tatiana's vegetable garden is tidy.

At the farm, Oleg asked me if I really want to continue my expedition – he has seriously offered that he and Nikolai come with me next year, using different horses. I have explained about my plans to ride from Karakorum (the ancient capital of Mongolia) to Hamburg, following in the steps of a monk called Giovanni di Plano Carpini who, in 1245, was sent out to spy on Ghengis Khan's successors. Although I had decided to hire horses in every country, we discussed using Mongolian ponies in Mongolia and camels in Kazakstan, and then maybe the Orlovs across Russia, Poland and Germany. I can't face all those documents again, however. I shall show them all to Nikolai and tell him that he must organize that side of it.

Anyway, having discussed it, we have agreed to forget it until I have returned to England and seen what reaction there is (or isn't).

There is a *Babushka*, or grandmother, here although I did not see her that first night. I have a little of her on video – tiny, with her soft, toothless brown face wrinkled like a sultana, brilliant blue eyes, and her hair, like everyone else's round here – permanently covered with the brightly-coloured scarf tied at the back of the neck.

Having got over her awe of the foreigner, she insists on talking to me in her thick accent and without any teeth. She told me she had had sixteen children and most had died, leaving her with one son in Kazakstan, where they used to live and two sons here. I met her coming out of the privy this afternoon – if she can still squat at her age, she is doing well.

I was stuck with her for about two hours while the others carried on working outside. She told me I spoke very 'clean' Russian, which I suppose in this context means 'clear'.

These people all seem to have taken me to their hearts, and I got a huge hug and kiss from Zeena when she left for Moscow, and Nikolai, Tatiana and the children all cluster round and talk to me, especially the youngest boy (also called Nikolai), who must be about twelve and makes the effort to finish my sentences when I get stuck, and corrects my grammar. I think he has given up his bed to me, as he is sleeping on a camp bed. The other beds are occupied by the other son, Vassily (aged just eighteen, a fat, silent, shy but pleasant enough lout), who claims to have spent seven years learning English at school but does not seem to know a word – and by Babushka.

I never did find out her name, but that's what everyone called her.

There is another young man, Sergei, and I can't quite figure out how he fits in. From something Babushka said, he may be the son of Nikolai's brother. Family relationships are so important here that there are specific terms for each. A sister-in-law, for example, is addressed differently if she is a husband's sister or a brother's wife. It is all much too complicated for me – at the moment I am concentrating on essentials like 'Take the right track by the cemetery' (an amazingly popular landmark), 'Keep straight on, leaving the sweet-corn on your left', 'There are wolves in that forest' and 'Did you see the traces of wild boar?' – phrases all unaccountably omitted from my guide book.

While waiting here, I have also had to learn the answers to: 'Do you make your own bread in England?' 'How much does flour cost?' 'Do you use yeast?' 'Do you also bottle tomatoes?' 'Can you milk a cow?' and 'Do you know how to make a Pizza?' 'Can you knit/sew?', plus an endless stream of 'In England do you have pears, mosquitoes, carrots, oak trees, wasps, apples, horse-flies, cabbages, foxes, sunflowers, wolves, potatoes, Colorado beetles, plums, cows, horseradish, sheep? . . .' In answer to the invariable question about whether our life is better than theirs, I have learned to make them laugh by saying 'It is very different, and I have to say our roads are much better!'. I also have to confess that I am not a typical Englishwoman in that I can (and do) make bread and milk a goat.

13 August – DAY 18
Nice day, but cold again. The Russian word for 'outside' actually

means 'on the street', which out here in the middle of nowhere, several miles from the nearest road, still makes me laugh. There are so few tarmac roads there that the word 'road' means track, and they have to specify 'asphalt' whenever they want to indicate what I would call a road.

Forgot my loo paper, which may cause a problem because in the privy there are two choices of newspaper, I *think* one is for used paper, but both of them are so filthy it is hard to see the difference! Must hunt round and find something.

Some friends dropped by – Serioje and his father. Upon meeting a foreigner, they rushed away to get some *Samagon*, [an extremely alcoholic, home-brewed Russian drink]. On the strength of that, Serioje took me into the woods to film – or so I thought! His hands were everywhere, and it was only thanks to my survival and self-defence training that I was not seriously alarmed. My lessons resulted in Serioje ending up horizontal, not I.

Eventually, after he staggered back on to his feet, I persuaded him to take me back to the farm, where he continued to push his luck and unfortunately, Tatiana was nowhere to be seen. I made it as plain as I could that I was not interested, but he told me he had never met a foreign woman before.

I told Tatiana afterwards that she had dangerous friends, and when I had explained what I meant we blamed it on the *Samagon*. [Tatiana told me two days later that she had heard he had been ill ever since and had had a fearful row with his wife. Nikolai was absolutely furious with him, and I never saw him again.]

I have underestimated Tatiana. She is intelligent, obviously loves her way of life, and looks extremely healthy and happy. She spoke last night with contempt of the German women, who sit watching television all day and, after watching her face for a while, I now see that a lot of her work is done for love, not just necessity. I seriously think she is the most contented woman I have ever met.

Have had to entertain Babushka for another couple of hours; today her speech was even harder to understand because Nikolai was operating a power-saw right outside the house. I have underestimated him, too – he actually does quite a lot of work outside. Apparently he will be forty soon, although I thought him older. Tatiana must be in her late thirties. I also learned from Babushka that Tatiana, too, had a daughter who died. Since nobody ever takes the slightest notice of Babushka, I am obviously condemned to play the part of willing listener for as long as I stay here.

Before Bannia, we had to round up all the little chicks, who seem to be considered old enough now to join the horses, cows, sheep, grown-up hens and turkeys in the shed next door, instead of sleeping in the ante-room of the Bannia. That took the best part of an hour. The three horses (two huge, working horses, one iron grey and one bay, plus a small one, which I think is a foal), have to my certain knowledge been stuck in the shed for over twenty-four hours, and quite likely for twenty-four weeks, with never any sign of being mucked out.

Tatiana then made some cheese. First I helped her and then I filmed the process. Before helping, I said I must wash my hands (having been scooping little chicks off filthy floors) but 'No need,' cried Tatiana. After that, dying of thirst, I risked, for the first time, having a drink out of the water churn, using the communal cup. Well, I am still taking the antibiotics, and it is delicious well water.

Giles rang. All is going well, and I also spoke to Ali. I have suggested I meet them in Minsk and guide them back to Stari Oskol, and I asked her to give me two days' notice as it will take me sixteen hours to get there by train.

NB: Of course, here I am marked as a foreigner the minute I produce a handkerchief – here, like further south and in Mongolia, you are supposed to blow your nose on the ground (or into the slop pail, if you happen to be indoors). Among the men, spitting seems obligatory, hawking is fortunately optional.

14 August – DAY 19

There is no doubt that I am still inhibited by the privy. In camp, I went to the loo as regular as clockwork as soon as I got up, whereas here it seems my body waits as long as possible! The privy is different from other systems too; beneath the hole in the floorboards, instead of a deep pit which gradually gets filled, I think there is a bucket which presumably (in theory) gets emptied, and it seems the done thing to put used loo paper into a bucket just under your nose.

Arman rang this morning, to my great surprise. He has either not seen the fax Giles sent to Anna (unlikely, but theoretically possible), or he is pretending everything is fine, as he asked

The photograph that really hit the press – hare-hunting with the Cossacks in October 1993

Where it all began – the Cossacks and their borzois

The first test-drive in Alexikovo 1994. I fell in love with Pompeii as we rode
through mile upon mile of empty snow-covered steppe

Masha and Malishka, best friends, but as wild as deer in winter 1994

A typical Russian country house

Ali stops in horror at the bridge. Many of the planks/trees were rotten –
Russia

Ali and I give the horses a drink – Russia

The Russian gypsies looked a bit rough, but were fascinated by my story!

Glorious Russian woods – Malishka is having a good roll

Above: The last evening at the farm in Stari Oskol, Russia. *Left to right:* Richard, Lena, me, Oleg, Tatiana, Zeena and Nikolai

Left: Making bread with Babushka on the Russian farm

Forests, bogs, wolves and ticks in Bryansk county

The famous Russian birch trees in Smolensk county

We help ourselves from a well in Belarus

Some Belarussian women 'interrogating' me

how I was, how things were going with the English party, and whether or not they had his home and office numbers in Moscow.

I am not sure what to do, and shall discuss it with Giles tonight. I am tempted to use him to meet the Brits and to guide them here, as I really do not fancy sixteen hours or more in a train. We could then send him back to Moscow or, if he behaves, I suppose he could, for a change, prove quite useful across Russia. *Pasmotrem.* ('We'll see'.)

I spent an hour helping Tatiana making *Pyelmyeny*, which we had for lunch with yummy garlicky sauce, and filmed a little using the remote control. This later fell down in the privy (not actually into the bucket, but somewhere invisible close at hand) – I simply could not face trying to retrieve it. Since I presume Richard Adamson's face is not to be made famous, I shall just ask him to film as much as possible, and might even ask Giles if he can replace the remote control in time.

Babushka said today that I spoke just like a Russian! I found out from Tatiana that Babushka is eighty-four and that she, Tatiana (with an eighteen-year-old son) is thirty-six. I also found out that young Sergei is the stepchild of her husband's brother.

11:30pm
Some very nice young neighbours came round, very anxiously enquiring in great secrecy if I can help them get to England and find work in the black economy. They are quite charming, and swore blind they were not afraid of hard work, but I really didn't know what to say, as I know nothing about it. I have promised to make enquiries, but, of course, I can do nothing.

Giles rang as usual. He is unhappy about using Arman (if by chance he hadn't seen Giles's fax when he rang and did later, would he take revenge by not turning up?), but I think I must go to Minsk anyway to get a new visa. I asked Giles if he could possibly find and send some batteries for a wonderful toy of young Nikolai's. It is an eight-language translator, including Russian and Polish. To my huge embarrassment, Nikolai (the father) later insisted on giving it to me as a present.

I learned last night that these people had been rich when in Kazakstan, and fully realise the primitiveness of their situation. I now know them quite well, but feel sure than an English couple in similar circumstances, within seconds of meeting a foreigner, would have pointed out that they had fallen on bad times.

Poor Nikolai has spent part of the last couple of days welding an iron fence and creating a small corral at the end of the half-built house due to my horses having eaten most of the original fence. It was ready this evening, so they were moved in there.

15 August – DAY 20

Pyelmyeny and sauce again for breakfast. I am eating as much garlic as I can to protect my stomach. Translated the instructions for the video machine from German to Russian, but for some reason it refuses to record.

At young Nikolai's request, I made a pizza for lunch, using what was available – tomatoes, onions, green peppers, cheese, garlic and dill. The dough did not rise well the first time, so I put the prepared pizza in a slightly warm oven. We cooked it when we could wait no longer, and the topping was quite tasty but the base was heavy – I should have started earlier. Maybe it will keep the boys from hankering after Western food.

To my great surprise, Anna Shubkina rang – she has tracked me down at last. She did not know much, and I got the impression she had not seen Arman. I told her the car was useless, not only did it get stuck in every puddle, but the gear box was bad and I had had to buy a new generator. I also told her exactly what I thought of Arman, and that Vassily had only wanted to flee from bandits – I really should have told her that at least he was kind and polite to me. She did not seem to know what had happened to Lev.

She wants Nikolai (Bezbatka) to go to the border to meet the Brits and bring them here, and will send a fax to Giles asking for details. The idea is that he will remain with us until we all get back to the Belarussian-Polish border. I like Nikolai and still think he at least is a professional – and I have not only paid in full for two months' use of the van and Arman, but also paid Nikolai US $400 (£265) for getting us across the border into Poland – so I am inclined to agree, but I told Anna that I want to discuss it with Giles.

In the meantime, poor Tatiana has spent most of the day trying to get through to the station to find out train times to Minsk, whether I would have to go via Moscow, etc. – just in case.

In the afternoon I went to pick mushrooms in the forest with Tatiana. This took us nearly three hours, long before the end of which I was bored and my back hurt. They are not worth it from my point of view, but I had heard that collecting mushrooms is a very important Russian hobby.

Nikolai's horses are now in the paddock where my horses were, and massive great creatures they are too. I take back all I have written, today the stable got cleaned out.

10:00pm
Giles has just rung. After some discussion, he agreed that Bezbatka should meet the Brits at the Kuznice-Grodno crossing and guide them here. They will be bringing proper bridles and saddles, and at my request Ali is also getting a selection of different sized girths.

16 August – DAY 21
Another bad night. I cannot decide if it is because I am too hot in bed, due to the flies which buzz round my face from dawn onwards, or raging sexual frustration.

On my return from my morning visit to the privy (either body or brain has decided not to be so fussy), it occurred to me that after weeks of not having a chain to pull, I might easily get out of the habit.

Was it Chekov or Tolstoy who was so sentimental about peasant life? The only difference I can detect between standards a century ago and standards now is that there seems to be electricity for all, television and/or telephone for some, and quite a few seem to have a lorry, car or tractor as well as horse-drawn transport. Listening to Babushka's story (and to a lesser extent Tatiana's according to Babushka), even the infant mortality rate hardly seems to have improved.

I spent a quiet morning studying. It's amazing how much better I retain new words in this environment. After a good lunch I helped to milk the cows, watched with amusement by the family. The one I milked had lost a quarter [one of her teats], which made it a bit confusing, but I managed to get most of her milk. Her teats were, of course, vast compared with those of Milou, my goat.

Then we set off to the market in town, where I got batteries for the translator (which is excellent, and even contains words such as 'graze', which I had not expected), a striped dark T-shirt and a denim skirt, which fits by some miracle. To my great delight, Tatiana also bought some fly-spray. By the time Nikolai had visited a couple of cronies on the way back it was gone 6pm. Nikolai was driving as usual – it seems that hardly any women out here can drive. Tatiana is astonished to hear that not only could I drive, but that Ali could as well and would share the driving with Richard.

Later
I helped Tatiana pick strawberries and carrots from the vegetable garden, and to round up the sheep, three of the flock apparently being under the illusion that a ewe in someone else's flock is their mother. Unfortunately, one of them, quite different in appearance from the others in that he somehow succeeds in looking like a miniature bison, is in love with one of the other ewes and didn't want to leave her. Judging by the amount of humping and fighting that I witnessed, they keep quite a lot of rams here.

Supper with quite a lot of vodka, then bed. Such bliss to have no flies.

17 August – DAY 22
Slept like a log – thanks to the vodka or fly-spray. Blissful breakfast, no flies, and Tatiana gave me the recipe for making condensed milk.

Last night Giles told me we have another day's delay because the Toyota did not have the spares, without which Richard dare not set out. I must continue to be patient and accept that here at least (unlike Moscow), my Russian fluency and comprehension, if not my accuracy, is improving in leaps and bounds. Tatiana keeps asking if I am homesick but, strangely, I am not at all. The only thing that brought a lump to my throat was a photograph of snowy mountains, which reminded me of the first three years of my life when I lived in the Alps. I must admit I would love a cup of decent coffee (they only have instant here, so I drink tea or water) and a large Scotch.

We searched for the instructions to the translating gadget in young Kolya's desk, which was very untidy. All his old essays, reports and paraphernalia were consigned to lavatory paper – no waste here. Tatiana also found some old photographs and the first one she showed me was of her daughter's funeral. I asked her how long ago it had happened, and she told me it was before little Kolya was born – so, at the age of twenty, she had a two-year old child and a dead child. Later I saw a photograph of another funeral, and in both cases I noticed the coffin was open for people to look at the body.

I also noticed that hulking great eighteen year old Vassily was hulking and huge at all ages. Husband Nikolai, on the other hand, photographed in various guises (including, of course, Army uniform) was very slim before he fell victim to Tatiana's cooking.

I am curious about Nikolai's brother, to whom I have never been formally introduced and whose name I don't know. He is here every day, working tirelessly, cutting pine logs into planks, but has never even been offered a cup of tea, let alone been allowed into the house. His wife, Nadia, frequently drops round, and his stepson, Sergei eats with us at lunch time. What is going on?

Sitting quietly in the sun I soon found myself surrounded by chickens and turkeys. No room for sentiment here as everything, with the possible exception of the cats and the two dairy cows, is destined for the pot.

That said, this family is less obsessed with meat than most Russians. In fact, I blame the Russian carnivorous lifestyle for the poverty of some of the areas I have ridden through. If they did not keep so much stock and overgraze the land, maybe they would not be so shockingly poor. This area here must be a very agricultural one – I have just seen an advertisement on television for special buckets for giving water to calves.

I made the mistake of thinking that a collection of cows seen together, with one man keeping an eye on them, is a herd. Maybe sometimes it is, but the families round here take it in turns to watch the cows, so Tatiana's four (two dairy, two young ones) go out with all the others every morning. They then come in at lunch time to rest and get milked for the second time before being turned out to pasture again in the afternoon, with the third milking being done in the evening.

I helped Tatiana with a mega wash-up of huge saucepans and cauldrons outside in the yard (where there *is* running water, I discovered). The usual cloths were not up to the job, so she calmly selected a stone and scrubbed the dirty pans with that. What century am I living in here?

Have just had a chat with Babushka and feel desperately sorry for her. Tatiana was rude and impatient with her earlier, and I found her in tears and felt moved to hug her. The poor old thing is a prisoner here. She did not really want to leave Kazakstan but was afraid to stay there with her other son (who has remained) because he drinks so much.

She has now changed her mind and wants to return, but it would be too expensive and, anyway, the other son has not replied to any of her letters. He does not have a telephone, although a neighbour does, but she does not know the number, and, in any case, the call would have to be booked. The difference in her way of life is enormous, and of course she has left all her friends behind. She must have been eighty-two when they moved here – very old for such an upheaval.

On the other hand, I can see Tatiana's point of view because the old lady is very querulous and constantly moaning about her headache or her back pains. In this country, however, respect for the old theoretically still holds and usually there are other daughters and daughters-in-law to share the burden of caring for Granny. Nikolai was her last child, so she must have been forty-four when he was born. When Tatiana is eighty-four, Vassily will be sixty-six and probably himself a grandfather.

Giles has rung – Richard and Ali should leave on Saturday morning. He had a fax from Anna in which she said she wants to come with Nikolai Bezbatka. Giles told her it would be uncomfortable in the back of the truck, but I told him that would not put her off and that I do not want her under any circumstances. If that means telling her straight, so be it.

When I told this to Nikolai and Tatiana, they laughed and agreed, and Nikolai actually said that, as a Russian, he was ashamed at the way my journey had suffered from such a lack of preparation and thought. He said this even though he has no idea how well-paid Anna had been for the job she had not done.

18 August – DAY 23

Big excitement of the week. On my routine morning visit to the privy, I found that it had been emptied. I must admit that the necessity of staring at a heap of stinking faeces had become no less daunting with custom.

Helping with the washing-up again, it occurred to me that

there are some advantages to this system – both the washer-up and dryer-up can do the job sitting down. Since there is no sink, we are by definition not tied to it and there is not very much to do as a rule since the most each person gets at a meal is a cup, a fork, occasionally a plate, and a teaspoon for tea. The tedium of the task is relieved for Tatiana by the excitement of events occurring in *Santa Barbara*, a typically awful American soap opera to which most Russians seem addicted and which has the benefit, from my point of view, of making everybody familiar with my name.

Sex, or rather the absence of it, is constantly on my mind, and leads me to wonder how on earth this married couple cope? There is no privacy here, no door between where they sleep and our dormitory, and anyone wanting a pee in the night has to go through their room. There is no lock on the door, and friends and neighbours drop in unannounced at all times of the day and night. Our dormitory, incidentally, is permanently dark as it has no window nor electric light, but seems to be about 10ft × 9ft.

Making some waffles while Tatiana does her evening chores, I decided to shut Babushka up by turning on the television. It was then I found out that everything in this kitchen is run off one socket with a three-way adaptor and that because I had the waffle iron (another rare gadget) plugged in, as well as the fridge and the kettle, the television was unplugged!

Early tomorrow morning the rescue party should be setting out, and I shall be so glad to see them. The horses and I are now rested, and ready to get on with our journey. To think I had originally hoped to be home by now, and we have only covered about 500–600 kilometres (310–370 miles) with at least 3,000 (1,860 miles) still to go. The team (taking turns at driving) ought to be able to do 800 kilometres (500 miles) a day, so just over three days' travelling, plus hanging around at Dover or wherever, plus queuing at borders. With any luck they might get here on Tuesday night. They can rest and we can pack my equipment on Wednesday, and leave on Thursday, God willing.

19 August – DAY 24
Early morning visit to privy brought a new horror: one of the baby chicks seems to have fallen into the pit and died, and then been shat on. Oh, yuck!

Drank two glasses of vodka *po-Russky* last night and was a bit tipsy when Giles rang, but confessed. Apparently the bit of film showing me downing a large stirrup cup in one slurp at Alexikovo when we left had been shown on ITN World News, so he was not surprised.

All well except that at the last minute I found they had not packed any HorseHage. I said it was very important and that I had hoped for ten or so bales but absolutely must have two or three in case I can't find any grass round Bryansk. I just dare not set out with none.

The other bit of bad news is that Anna continues to insist on coming, and apparently she and Nikolai plan to follow in their own car, so comments about the amount of room available in the truck are, of course, irrelevant. If she does come here it will be very awkward, but I shall try to send her home. Her people did their best to ruin this venture, and I have accepted Nikolai only because I hope and believe he will do a good professional job, but I won't have Anna running round and bossing everyone about. If she is deaf to all subtle hints and even outright requests for her to go, then I shall simply ignore her. Trust her to go and try to bugger up my life again. Maybe this is to be another test for my new-found assertiveness.

Stomach warnings sent me running first for my medication, then to the privy. It is impossibly unhygienic here when every dish is shared and all water scooped out of the churn with one mug – then either drunk by somebody or used to fill the kettle – and with all the food covered with flies. I cannot help but notice(!) that everyone here has permanent slight diarrhoea, so it is not just my feeble constitution. Giles would die in a week after his gut trouble from military service.

Browsing through *The Oxford Book of Exploration*, I feel more and more inadequate, but was amused by the quotation from Samuel Butler, 'Exploring is delightful to look forward to and back upon, but it is not comfortable at the time, unless it be of such an easy nature as not to deserve the name'. I was slightly shocked at Wilfred Thesiger's remark about his crossing of the Rub'al-Khali on a camel before it was possible to cross it in a car, writing, 'to have done the journey on a camel when I could have done it in a car would have turned the venture into a stunt'. Is my venture then only a stunt? Be honest. Yes, perhaps he is right. Nowadays there is almost nowhere left in the world which is inaccessible to machines, in my very limited experience only in the High Altai mountains of Mongolia was horseback the only means of travel, so anyone with any sort of spirit of adventure is forced to create artificial circumstances as I have done. Is it not better to do a stunt than to sit at home watching television? Whatever personal and spiritual satisfaction I may achieve will surely be no less than had the combustion machine never been invented.

One might as well say that now it is possible to buy bread and vegetables, there is no point in making or growing your own; wonderful music is readily available on CD, so it's a waste of time learning to play an instrument, and with whole libraries now stored on computers, why buy a real book and actually read it in an old-fashioned paper form?

On a practical level, how else could I travel at leisure through this, or any other country, looking into people's gardens, observing the wildlife that flees from cars but not from horses, or pausing to chat to the curious locals? Had I just stuck the horses in a lorry and driven them back home, there is no way I would have been able to spend so much time with this kind family and observe so minutely their way of life.

Is the lady protesting too much?

At my request, Giles had made enquiries about somewhere for the horses to rest for a day or two after crossing into Poland. Amazingly, Ali has a friend who knows a Pole who just happens to be mad on horses and just happens to be reasonably well off and just happens to speak English and just happens to live near Byalistok.

Had a rest and then had some delicious home-made condensed milk, and some tea. The result was that I felt incredibly sweaty and sick. I am annoyed that the two little toes on my right foot have had very little sensation for some weeks – is the riding itself to blame, the boots, or the lack of walking?

A note on mucking out (or not) – I think I may again have misjudged. I noticed a few days ago that the corral (about three times the size of an average English loose-box), in which my three horses live, seemed amazingly clean, so I kept watch for a while. There are so many chickens and other scavengers here that droppings instantly attract a dozen or more birds who peck and scuffle the dung into powder form. On further inspection, I found the same applies to the shed next door, where Nikolai's two vast draught horses and five month old foal share an area rather smaller than a racehorse's stable.

One of Kolya's friends has just taken me for a ride on his cart, so I could see how the horses here are driven. He told me that the horse, aged eleven, was very old – so the hard work they have to do certainly shortens their life-span. When I told him my Arab was twenty-one, he nearly collapsed in astonishment. Had I looked more closely at the cart, I should never have made the request, as we trotted across the grass it was difficult to decide whether the planks forming the cart would disintegrate before or after the wheels fell off. Helping Tatiana with the laundry (whenever she did the washing, an ancient twin-tub washing machine appeared), I noticed again that in Russia the sheets are always too small. They are invariably too short – when I was in Moscow I had a single sheet on the double bed, so of course it was also too narrow. On the other hand, the pillows are huge (about a metre square). They also have a different system for blankets, using something like a duvet cover for these, but instead of the opening being at the bottom, there is a decorative hole about one foot square in the middle of the cover, through which the blanket is inserted and remains visible.

Did some ironing on the kitchen table, while Babushka asked if we did ironing in England. I sometimes think that, apart from the fact that I share these people's skin colour and general features, I am as strange to them as if I had come from a different planet. Although they sit glued to *Santa Barbara*, these people do not seem to connect the ritzy way of life in that programme with this scruffy foreigner in jeans and a T-shirt.

20 August – DAY 25

After a couple of glasses of *Samagon* last night, I was relieved to wake without a hangover – the ghastly stuff must actually be quite pure. It occurs to me that the Russian way of downing your glass in one may have come about through having to force down foul, home-brewed stuff – the alcohol kicks in before you get the taste!

Giles rang. The reason he didn't ring last night was that the team only left at 8pm British time. I was disappointed, said so, and then he felt guilty, but I had thought they were setting out at dawn, not dusk. Yet another day's delay – oh, hell. They should be nearly into Poland by now.

So I sit and wait, and cheerfully allow myself to be used – not as an unpaid slave, but as a slave who is paying heavily for the privilege. Not fair, of course, as I do not have to do anything, and anyway, we have not agreed a rate. I hope they don't play the same trick as Zeena and refuse to accept anything, but on the other hand, US $20 (£13) a day really would be too much, although they are very short of money and have been incredibly kind to me.

Reading again, I see that Frank Kingdon-Ward made exactly the same comments as I have about the local (in his case, Tibetan) attitude to animals, '. . . they are not unkind. Simply, they live hard lives themselves, and expect their animals to follow their example and take stoically what comes next'.

I have just had a visit from a couple of local women – it seems the grandson of one and nephew of the other, ten years old, has been blind from birth. If I understood correctly, some part of his eyes are actually missing. They want to know if a transplant can be done in England because they have been told by doctors in Moscow that it is possible, but not in Russia. I said I had no idea but I would find out, and they will bring him tomorrow. I am not sure I want to look too closely at someone with essential bits missing, but here, too, is a test and I must not fail.

When Giles rings I must ask him to find out, and I have asked for a proper diagnosis so I can give him all the information. Can I get publicity for them so they don't have to find what would, for them, undoubtedly be a huge amount of money?

Interestingly they say there is another child in the region (a fourteen year old girl) with exactly the same defect. Surely more than average? Is Chernobyl to blame?

21 August – DAY 26

I have been considering the way of life here, and how easy it would be to get sentimental. I caught myself thinking yesterday (I was helping Tatiana wash pots at the time) that really there is a lot to be said for a simple, rustic existence. Why do we surround ourselves with expensive luxuries? This life is not so bad really. I then reminded myself sharply that washing pots in cold water may be OK in the summer sunshine, but how would it feel in the depths of the famous Russian winter?

All the same, I would hate to think that in a few years' time every peasant here lived as we in England do – having everything, yet never satisfied. All these people really need is safer electricity, indoor loos and hot and cold running water and money (apparently employers here try very hard to make their employees take their wages – the average wage in Russia being less than US $50 (£33) a month – in sugar or flour).

I did also point out to Tatiana and to Sergei that we are nothing like as free as they are. Firstly, we have a million regulations that we have to obey and secondly, every square inch of our country belongs to somebody, so we cannot do as they do, which is walk or ride wherever we like, graze our animals wherever we like, fish in any pond or river that takes our fancy, pick mushrooms wherever we find them, cut grass from the meadows for hay when we need it, or take our guns and / or dogs and kill whatever we need for food.

At this they were amazed. I feel as strongly as ever that our freedom in England has been almost completely eroded, and that in my view it is too high a price to pay for our extremely comfortable way of life. I do not want a dishwasher or tumble-dryer so badly that I am prepared to sacrifice the joy and safety of riding along tracks or through woods. I am not sure I want to continue to live in a country where Nanny State interferes with every aspect of my daily life – wear protective headgear, put on your safety-belt, don't smoke, don't drink, butter is bad for you, do not cross the railway line, do not go out in the sun, and more. At the same time, Nanny State will not subsidize the railways but spends zillions on roads, and seems to encourage the over-use of pesticides instead of helping organic farmers.

Ura Prisheppa rang late this morning to say that my saviours will cross into Belarus tomorrow and be here the day after. That surprised me, as I should have expected them to be almost at Byalistok by now, but maybe there were long queues at Frankfurt-am-Oder. He further surprised me by saying that Bezbatka will meet them and bring them here, then return to Moscow, and did I want Arman to accompany us thereafter? I had to think fast, but decided that Arman was worse than nobody and I really never wanted to see him again, so declined the offer. 'Who will interpret?' Ura wanted to know. 'I shall do it myself', I told him.

I forgot to mention that there *is* a window between the kitchen and the dormitory, but I did not notice it at once because for some reason it is covered with black-out material. There is also another window in the kitchen, facing east, which is covered with thick brown paper. Why?

The family with Aliosha, the blind child, arrived but the video battery had run down. The charger, of course, is with my other luggage which I had hoped would be restored to me yesterday. I have been promised I shall have it tonight, so Aliosha will be produced again tomorrow. Poor kid, he is naturally timid and very afraid in strange places. I now gather he is completely without eyes, and, although he kept his lids closed the whole time, it certainly looked as if the sockets were empty. He was born just after Chernobyl, but Tatiana and I thought there was probably no connection as he would surely have been fully formed two or three weeks before birth. Apparently his mother was ill in the tenth week of pregnancy, but they assured me it was definitely not German Measles.

Baking hot again – too hot to sunbathe after a while, so sought shade while reading about Sven Hedin almost dying of thirst in the desert. Think I shall turn to the section covering the Arctic and Antarctic to cool myself down. After resting, went to the privy to find yet another horror – a baby chicken dying in the pit. I ran to tell Tatiana who went to have a look, pronounced it dead, and tried to build a barrier to prevent chicks falling in again (the previous barrier having been lost when the pit was emptied). Returning for my delayed pee, I found the chick still in death-struggles. I could not reach it, there was nothing to be done, but although I was desperate, there was no way I could pee on that chick. Tatiana thought it frightfully funny that I should be so sentimental, pointing out that I did not have to look at it. So I waited in the kitchen for three-quarters of an hour with my legs crossed in agony, until I was absolutely certain the poor scrap was dead.

After a couple of tots of vodka, Nikolai and I planned the next trip. He wants to send Orlovs to Mongolia by train and use the same (branded) horses for the whole trip. I expressed doubts about crossing the High Altai on anything but a native pony, but he is sure they can do it. I remain dubious, having been there. But there is no doubt it would be a wonderful advertisement for the Orlov – crossing the mountains in spring, the heat of Kazakstan in summer, then Russia in the autumn and the winter snows, then Poland and Germany. He thinks we need five horses and five mad enthusiastic people who would do the trip for free.

I said I had sworn never to take a horse over a bureaucratic border again, but he pointed out that Mongolia to Kazakstan and Kazakstan to Russia would involve minimal paperwork. The next worry is that, although the horses would originate west of the Urals (apparently very important from the EC point of view), the journey will start east of the Urals.

Giles rang and there is some confusion as to where the Team had got to. He said he would ring Anna or her father and ring me back if they had any news. I also explained about the eyeless child and he promised to make enquiries of his doctor friend, Paul McLoughlin, and let me know.

22 August – DAY 27

At breakfast Nikolai said he would like us to work together on selling horses (Orlov or Danskai) to Poland, Germany, France and England, and told me to think about it and discuss it with Giles when I get home. We got quite carried away with the thought of me driving a *Troika* [a cart with three horses] round Newmarket Heath. He says it is quite difficult and he will teach me. Nikolai also told me last night that when travelling through thick, driving snow, they put the horses in Indian file (which they call *Goosem*, which comes from the word 'goose') to make it easier.

Young Kolia was sent out mid-morning with an airgun to shoot a cockerel, but when I went outside to clean my boots, I found him with live cockerel in hand, offering to let me kill it. I declined and remembered an urgent appointment elsewhere. At his insistence I had a go at a tin can with the airgun, but to my shame only hit it with the second pellet.

In the kitchen, Babushka was plucking the cockerel and Tatiana was washing up. As I dried, I found nine glasses and asked if they had had a party after I had gone to bed. They laughed and Tatiana told me that she had decided to clean all the glasses in honour of the British visitors.

She is also having a thorough spring clean, including putting net curtains up at the kitchen window and the one formerly covered with black-out material. Even the paper has been taken off the east window. Maybe, without proper curtains, the purpose was to keep the early morning summer sun from waking them too early.

I was woken from my afternoon nap by Tatiana telling me the

police were here to see me. A rather good-looking young man asked to see my passport and all the other documents. He spent ages studying my passport and asked a lot of questions, including the inevitable, 'Why?' He pointed out that my visa was for Moscow only, and for the purpose of learning the Russian language. I explained that I had told the travel agent exactly where I was going and what I was doing on this trip.

In the end, very nicely, he pointed out that I should have registered with some local authority, that I should do so without delay, and that I and the Myelnikov family would have to pay a fine. I thought I heard Nikolai mutter something to Vassily about 'two million' (approximately £300), which may be the amount we each have to pay, and of course I must pay theirs, too. Am tempted to drop Shubkina in it by telling the relevant authorities that, when I enquired about registering when I was in Moscow, she told me it was quite unnecessary.

Aliosha and his family turned up and I filmed him as best I could.

Still no idea where the Brits are. . . .

11pm
Giles rang. He has not heard anything either and is going mad with worry. I told him we would certainly have heard if there had been a problem. We both hope they arrive tomorrow. Giles thinks the Russians may not have turned up in time and that the Brits are alone in the middle of nowhere, but I said that had the Russians not turned up, Richard would certainly have rung me, explained the situation, and asked for directions to the farm. I also pointed out how time-consuming it was to find an inter-city telephone in this country.

Giles also told me that, after extensive enquiries and ringing a couple of the country's most senior ophthalmologists, it turned out that the story of eyeless people receiving eye transplants had been widespread a few years back, but that it was all a cruel hoax. Now I or Tatiana must break the news to Aliosha's family.

Spoke to Katie and suggested she spend a week or so riding across Poland – she seemed pleased.

23 August – DAY 28

Woke early because the sun, undimmed by brown paper, was streaming onto my face. There was a rush of activity because Nikolai and Tatiana were off to visit a neighbour of her mother's who is staying nearby and will take back messages and letters to Germany when she returns on Thursday.

Last night we had *borscht* and I can report with authority (this being my second experience of the famous Russian dish) that beetroot is either insignificant or totally missing. The first *borscht* I had at Zeena's had none, and while helping to prepare the vegetables last night, I noted that there was only one very small beetroot, one cabbage, three carrots, three onions and about 2lb of potatoes, all of which were added to the pot in which the chicken was boiling. Sadly, everything here is boiled, or occasionally fried. The only time the gas oven has been switched on was the day I made pizza.

Vassily, after nearly a fortnight, is losing his shyness and starting to talk to me other than in grunts and monosyllables. Better late than never.

Tried to rest after lunch, unsuccessfully because I knew we had to go and register with police. Here we endured a classic Russian situation. Before we could talk to the police 5,500 roubles (US $1.50) had to be paid in at a bank, but the first three banks were either closed or in some other way not functioning. At last, after success at the fourth bank, we dashed back to the police station, but were told, 'Sorry, it is too late now, and we are closed tomorrow (Thursday) so please come back on Friday'. 'But we are leaving on Friday'. 'In that case, come back tomorrow at 10am, it will take some time. Meanwhile, please fill in this form . . .'

Back to the farm, no Brits, no news. Tried to rest, but Giles rang. He also has no news and is tearing his hair out. I tried to reassure him, but he won't rest till they are here. I must admit I am getting a little worried – if only they had rung.

Big news of the day (failing Brits' arrival) is that at last I have made friends with the dog. What a relief!

I sit and wait and worry about my friends and about the police. I discussed the situation with Tatiana and we have agreed I should explain that, when I raised the subject of registration when in Moscow, I was told it was not necessary and not to worry. It is not that I particularly want to dump Anna in the shit, but that I want to protect myself (the nice policeman is ex-KGB).

She has done me no good at all and charged me a vast amount of money, so why should I protect her?

24 August – DAY 29
Hallelujah – the Brits arrived at 12.30am. I was fast asleep and not with it at all, but I fed and watered them. Bezbatka and Anna left at once, saying Nikolai had to be in Moscow by 10am. Nikolai Myelnikov reckoned they were just ashamed. He also said later it was the height of bad manners not to accept so much as a cup of tea before rushing away.

Back to sleep, and have had all day to catch up with Ali and get to know Richard, who I think will do very well. Richard loaded as much of my equipment as he felt he needed on to the truck, but we had to make some sacrifices, such as the barbecue and chemical loo (which I would never have used anyway) and quite a bit of food, and pots and pans which I hope will be useful to the family.

I should just describe my rescuers. Ali is thirty-two years old, tall and blond, and very beautiful. Richard is also quite tall, aged fifty-five, with grey hair and very fit-looking (time will tell if he really is fit). He announced today that he was considering growing a beard, and my response was, 'You'll never get a better opportunity'.

Giles had also sent out, at my suggestion, a vast stock of presents for my hosts, and photocopies of a few pages from Mrs Beeton because I want to teach Tatiana to make her own sweets. Russian confectionery is not very good, and the foreign stuff is, of course, too expensive for ordinary people to buy. I therefore had to spend an hour or so translating the recipes into Russian, but unfortunately most of them require cream of tartar and/or essences which are simply not available here. So when I get home I must send Tatiana some of those little luxuries.

CHAPTER SIX

Off Again

25 August – DAY 30

What a difference. We got up early to say goodbye to Nikolai who was off at 7am, we packed, tacked up, and I paid for the horses' keep and my own, left enough money for the KGB fine (about US $450 [£300]) in case they had to pay both lots (I told Tatiana it could be a down payment on the first Orlov if she did not have to pay the fine). She tried to prevent me paying for my keep but I firmly told her that everything had been agreed with Oleg.

There were tearful farewells and we were off. During the day I endured no dramas, no sulks, no resentment, just lots of laughs and fun – bliss. We retraced the steps of my last riding day, except Richard found much better tracks. They are beginning the harvest now so instead of huge fields of sunflowers we are seeing more fallow land. There is still plenty of meadowland and we continue to see acres of sweet-corn, but I suspect that will soon be harvested. One lucky aspect of the various delays is that the oats have been cut, and Nikolai assured me we would have no problem buying it on the journey.

Our first campsite was OK but not perfect as there were loads of mosquitoes and we were right by the railway line, but the grazing (the most important consideration) was fine. I hope we continue to be able to find trees in which to camp – it has been no problem up to now, and I for one feel less exposed when the truck is reasonably well concealed.

26 August – DAY 31

I woke at 4am, and heard twigs cracking but didn't know if it was bandits, Richard or a horse moving around, so I went back to sleep. Richard woke us at 6.10am and brought me coffee in bed (a bivvy-bag which he brought; it is brilliant and so much quicker to put up than a tent). I think Masha may be coming into season – oh damn. [Of course, had we but known it, she must have been four months pregnant by this stage.]

Another good day: Richard is brilliant at navigating. Ali had lost her saddle-saver last night, and search as we may, it was never found. She has had to use another numnah on top of the saddle instead. [A saddle-saver goes over the saddle to prevent the rider getting saddle-sores.]

We forded the Oskol river at a beautiful spot with willows and poplars everywhere, and part of the river fenced off to let the cattle drink. The truck got stuck in very deep sand on the other side of the river, but Richard soon got it out.

After beginning on tracks, we had to return to the roads after lunch. Ali had trouble with a couple of drunken amorous youths, who then turned their attention to me when they could not make themselves understood. They were vastly intrigued – like all Russians – at the sight of two women riding, plus there was the added curiosity of leading a spare horse. They made life quite awkward for a while, but we managed to get rid of them. Then, in the last village we passed through, a motor-bike slowed down when it passed us, so I put up my hand to say thank you and this display of manners caused the driver to stop, thinking I had hailed him.

Also while riding through that last village we spotted piglets disporting themselves like puppies. Everyone in the Russian countryside keeps pigs, but they are invariably confined to a shed and are seldom seen. These piglets were a joy to behold because they were themselves so joyful.

The mares were rather listless today – was the worming we had done two days ago taking its toll? Richard chose a campsite beside a lovely big lake, but Ali and I felt it was much too exposed (it was not only visible from the road but also too close to a village where they were having a party). She and I selected a new one a little further on, which was lovely but, being in a hollow, there were hordes of mosquitoes.

The countryside continues to be slightly undulating and just plain vast. Were it not for the *passadki* which line literally every road, and the occasional small copses, it would be dreary indeed – as it is I still revel in it.

Delicious supper again. I must say Ali cooks wonderfully and imaginatively combining packet and tinned food, and the results of Richard's shopping. He is having a bad time already – because most country people are self-sufficient it is very hard to buy the basics like tomatoes, cheese or meat.

For the Russians, bread seems to have a significance far beyond just food. If stocks of bread are running low, something approaching panic sets in until more bread is found. I noticed this with Arman and with Zeena, whose kitchen never had less than about four loaves of bread. It is possible to buy bread, although it is often stale.

27 August – DAY 32
Richard woke me soon after midnight: 'We've got a problem, the police are here'. I got up, went over and greeted them. There was a car with a blue flashing light parked on top of the hollow and searchlights pointing at us. I apologized, thinking it was forbidden to camp here. Oh no, that is not the problem, they said. There is the pond, and in the pond there are fish. . . Aha, I said, I understand (although I was amazed to think it was forbidden to fish). Everyone was very good-humoured, and it ended with laughs all round, especially when I told them where we were going on horseback.

This was a watershed. I realized after they had gone, smiling broadly at our expedition, that I had actually held the whole conversation without really having to think about the language. Could not get back to sleep for hours. I was very cold as stupidly, in order to see the stars, I left my head out of the bivvy bag where the dew could (and did) settle!

Richard had locked the car keys in the cab, so he had to take the Truckman top off (no mean feat, even with our help) and get in through the rear window. Ali told me that this had happened in Berlin on the outward journey, but on that occasion she had had the spare pair with her. Needless to say this time her spare keys were in her jacket in the cab. I was left with the impression that Ali felt that Richard had been careless.

In the morning we had another visit from the police but I smoothed it over by flirting like mad, which seems to be a very successful ploy in this country. Later, after we had set out, a total lunatic accosted us on the road, and grabbed hold of Pompeii's bridle. I was quite concerned, as short of knocking him out I could not see how to get away from him, but one of last night's police came to the rescue. Richard caught us up very late but all was OK.

The weather is still very hot.

At the very end of the day came the first seriously nasty incident of the trip. We were accosted by three drunk youths on a motor-bike. I knew we were in for trouble when I heard the foul language they were using. One of them tried to grab Pompeii's bridle, and another tried to pull me out of the saddle, so I galloped off. Malishka, whom I was leading, stopped dead, so I had to let go (this was not a suitable moment to be dragged out of the saddle). The youth was about to grab her lead rein when Ali rode at him yelling and, I'm sorry to say (well, not very sorry), that Masha, now steel-shod, trampled on him and we all galloped away, with Malishka running free. About half a mile on we met Richard. He realized something was wrong and hesitated, so I shouted 'Just go!' and, bless him, like a good Marine he didn't hesitate or ask questions but went, and we trotted to a lovely campsite.

Richard was very upset that we had experienced two nasty incidents today and he had not been present on either occasion. I pointed out that I had never expected (or even wanted) a permanent bodyguard, and that it is much more important for him to be on hand if necessary during the night, to scout out the way, to find campsites, and to do our shopping. I also reminded him that one of the many things Arman did which so annoyed me was being constantly around, either driving behind me, or, if he did go ahead, I would find the van round every corner waiting for me.

We hid the horses in the woods as best we could, and our hearts sank when a motor bike with a side-car rolled up. The rider seemed a nice bloke, and we thought he was probably a local farmer, so I apologized if we were camping illegally. He asked where we had come from (I named a town about ten kilometres back), and where we were going to (I said to Tym, which is the next town to the west).

We had hardly finished eating when it started to rain. It is now 10pm and I am exhausted. Richard, bless him, has gone into sentry mode, as we are all very uneasy at the thought that the drunken motor cyclists, after picking up their injured friend, might easily follow our tracks to our camp. After all, my horses are probably the only shod ones in the whole country, so their hoof prints are easy to distinguish.

28 August – DAY 33

Awoke at 4am and had a slight panic because I couldn't find the zip to undo my bivvy bag. Lovely starlit night. At 6 it started raining again. Feel sure Richard was on the alert all night. Got going slowly (everything was wet, although the rain had stopped by the time we were ready), and I rode off with all three horses while Richard, who was riding with me, fetched the Toyota out of the wood for Ali to drive. It was about twenty minutes before I remembered that the passenger seat in the truck was completely filled by the fridge. I stopped and the truck came along with Ali sitting on the roo-bar. She said afterwards that the expression on the faces of the oncoming drivers had been price-less: 'So this is how the Westerners carry their women.'

Pompeii had a warble-fly bite on his back so I rode Malishka (now renamed Muffin because she can be so mulish), and Richard rode Masha. Richard is not riding fit, and the ground was seriously soggy, so there was no trotting today.

We stopped in Tym for fuel and were halted by the police who wanted to see our documents, but when these were produced they lost interest. They mentioned a motor bike, so we guessed last night's farmer had reported us. Had it been the drunken youths no doubt we would have been in deep trouble for injur-ing one of them.

I am beginning to think that being my own interpreter has many advantages. First and foremost, I actually know what is going on, which was something I never did when Arman was around. Also, I feel certain that our path is made much smoother because the police who stop us have no axe to grind. Instead of other Russians over whom they might well feel the need to pull rank, they are having to deal with someone who is not only a woman, but a foreigner to boot. How can they pull rank on me?

A word about our routine – we are much busier than I had ever imagined. In the evenings, when we get to the camp-site Richard has chosen, he puts out the tethers for the horses and we untack and tie them up. Then Richard unpacks the truck, lights a fire, puts up the awning and feeds the horses – I don't usually do it because he won't let anyone else have access to the truck. Ali does the cooking and I put up the bivvy-bags. After supper somebody (usually Richard) does the washing up. By that time we are all pretty tired and it is dark, so I go to bed.

In the mornings my alarm goes off at 5.15am and, if Richard hasn't beaten me to it, I feed the horses (Richard having prepared the feeds the evening before). Most mornings are heaven – Richard has not only beaten me to it but brings us a cup of tea in bed. Then we dress, have breakfast (porridge cooked by Richard, or muesli), wash up, take down bivvy-bags, stuff sleeping bags back into sacks (my most hated job), let air out of mattresses and so on. Richard does not like anyone else to pack the truck so we usually help him fold up the awning before setting off on the horses, leaving him to finish loading. On most days he catches us up within an hour or so and goes on ahead to scout.

29 August – DAY 34
We are all too slow about getting going, and have agreed we must either move faster or get up earlier. Left at 8am. I rode Muffin and Ali was on Masha. We got on very well to start with (we are back on tracks, thank goodness) and did lots of trotting. We obtained water from some peasants in a tiny village – buckets of water for the horses were drawn from a large pond, and water for us from a well. The locals were charming, but clearly thought we must have come from outer space!

After much thought, I have decided to tell the locals the truth about our destination, as it seems silly to pretend that we, obviously foreigners, are riding from the last village to the next one. I suppose my thinking had been contaminated by my timid Russian helpers.

All the tracks were wet, so Richard had a lot of problems with the Toyota, culminating in being hauled out of what looked like a giant puddle but must have been the village pond. All the locals crowded round, fascinated to hear about our journey. One chap, driving a lorry, desperately wanted a souvenir of our passage. 'What can I show my grandchildren to prove I met you?' (he was about twenty). Sadly, the Polaroid had been left at Tatiana's and I had nothing else to give.

We stopped in the next large town and tried to buy some cheese. The shopkeeper directed us to a white house, but 'Nyet', said the guardian, 'we only sell to special people'. 'But we are on a long journey', I protested. 'Nyet, but if you wait for an hour the bus will come'. Baffled by this, we went to try the post office to ring Sasha to give news to Giles.

We covered about eighteen kilometres, then Richard found some lovely grazing for lunch. Hot as hell again.

30 August – DAY 35
Off at 7.30am. We became not exactly lost, but unable to cross assorted streams and rivers that Richard had thought we could get through while he went round the long way by road. In desperation I even tried leading Pompeii (brave horse) over a rusty rickety iron plank which was masquerading as a bridge, but it was no good because we could not get any further. This is one occasion when the walkie-talkie brought by Richard really proved its worth, because Richard had no idea we had had to turn back. After making contact, we met him by a truly beautiful lake, and continued by road. Pompeii's back is still oozing pus from the warble-fly bite, although it is much better, so I continue to ride the mares. Because I am lighter than Ali, we always swap at lunch time, so neither mare has to carry her greater weight all day.

Eventually we came to the road we wanted, and had lunch beside it. It was very hot again. Into the town of Svobodna, we rode through the streets, over the river, and up a very steep hill. There was a stunningly beautiful church at the top of the hill which had been visible for miles. We had also noted, from a distance, a building that resembled a mixture of Bavaria and Disneyland with its pointed towers and parapets. We passed right beside the church which we could see had just been restored, and I was told it was celebrating its 700th birthday. It was a fairly typical Russian church as one sees in the big cities – white and blue, with the traditional gold onion domes, but most of the churches I have seen so far in the countryside have been in a very sorry state of complete decay.

In the centre of Svobodna we found Richard struggling with a policeman who seemed to think we had to go to Kursk because it was in his and Ali's outward itinerary. I eventually managed to explain that we were on the return journey and that, with the horses, we were afraid of large towns. In other words, I flirted my way out of trouble once more. We caused a huge stir.

Met my policeman eight kilometres out of town again, and he gave further directions and wished us a good journey.

31 August – DAY 36

Up early, left at 7am. Did nearly sixty-four kilometres, but not quite because Masha was very tired. Why? I felt certain she was the best horse. We later discovered that the more oats she had, the more she flagged, contrary creature! Pompeii is still dragging my arm off, but he seems to have learnt that if he comes forward and slackens the rope before turning to bite the flies on his back, I don't shout quite so loudly at him.

The day started on roads. We took water fairly early and a very nice man invited us to help ourselves to sugar-beet. I said, 'Thank you, we would love a bit for the horses' to which he replied, 'Take a few hectares'.

Later on, riding across country, we were chased after by a young man on his horse (which we found a bit alarming at first because we couldn't run away from him), who wanted to know everything as usual. We ended up swapping stirrup irons, so when I have found my Timberland boots I can wear them, the stirrups Ali brought from England being too narrow.

We suffered a rainstorm late in the morning, and picked some corn on the cob for the horses' supper.

The weather warmed up after lunch, but there was still a nice fresh breeze, so we had no problems with sweaty horses.

Towards the end of the day we crossed the border out of Kursk *oblast* (county), so we have crossed the whole region in a week.

Unfortunately the last village through which we travelled was horrid. It was grim and filthy, and some very unpleasant-looking men came up when we watered the horses at the village pond – both Ali and I felt extremely uneasy, even though Richard was with us. We could not go quite as far from the village as we would have liked because Masha was flagging, so we are now camped in a hollow, which we thought was nicely hidden until a tractor came round and spotted us – damn.

I do hope Masha improves so we can really get a move on, although tomorrow is a day off. We cannot stay here because we are too close to that unpleasant village, but Richard says there should be another site about six kilometres away. After we have moved, we can go shopping.

1 September – DAY 37

We woke to our first frost and it took us hours to warm up. I dug out my fur hat, cashmere pullovers, silk underwear and scarves.

Rode about seven kilometres to a perfect campsite – a green glade in the forest, well away from the road, well hidden and with masses of lovely grazing. Pompeii is still having problems with the bite on his back but it is getting much better. Ali rode Masha with a headcollar instead of the bridle, as that horse really fights the bit anyway. Ali coped very well, but she had trouble stopping Masha with no bit.

We washed all our clothes, then Ali and I drove to Orel. The first filling station we stopped at had no diesel, the second one had it, but the first pump we tried had no hose, but we got there in the end. I had some money returned as I had mistakenly paid for petrol, which is more expensive than diesel – these Russians are so honest.

We stopped to buy tomatoes at the roadside, but the old women selling them had no scales and we didn't want a whole bucketful! We drove empty-handed into town where (due to a dearth of signposts), I had to ask where the centre was, but nobody knew. We finally found it, but unfortunately we could not call England from the post office, although I was able to change money there. I was directed to another building to make my phone call. I booked and paid for five minutes, and waited for forty. The call was announced so I rushed to one of the phone booths and then five minutes of shouting 'hello' (literally, as I was afraid they would charge me and kept checking my watch) and I got through to Giles. The line was even more truly awful than usual, and I am still not sure how much he heard [not a lot, he told me later].

Gave him various messages (it sounded like a shopping list, I fear). He sounded strained, so I asked what the problem was. It seems my old Arab mare, Aysha (one of the calmest horses in England) had reared up on being led from her stable and had to have seven stitches in her head. He assured me that she was fine now. He took the stitches out this morning and it seems the only lasting effect is that she now wants her forehead scratched all the time. Also he has had a row with the local farm foreman about where he walks the dogs, which to me riding freely across the countryside out here seems so indescribably petty.

So one hour later I got back to Ali, who had decided to wait in the truck. After another two hours we had bought food but no small-scale maps (the shop had run out of them). I also wanted to get some blankets, because Ali is cold at night, but we could not find any shop selling such things, and we were running very short of time. In the end I went for broke and asked in the hotel, outside of which we had parked the car: 'Excuse me, we are English, we cannot find the right shop and we need some blankets because we are so cold – can we buy some of your old ones?' 'Nyet' was the knee-jerk response but, when I pleaded, the receptionist obviously realised she might profit by these nutty foreigners. Calls were made to the *dijornaya* and two beautiful blankets were produced for $20 (£13). These thoughtful people even wrapped the blankets in a sheet in case we had problems carrying them to the car. Needless to say, they were riveted to hear about our journey.

We had told Richard we expected to return between 4 and 5pm, but by the time we got back to camp it was 8pm, and Richard had spent the last two hours deciding what he would do when we didn't turn up! As he pointed out, what would we have done, had we had a crash? How could we have communicated with him if we had any kind of problem?

We were very tired but there was still lots to do (move the horses, feed them, unload the truck, set up our bivvy-bags, eat), so now it is after 11pm and we have still not done everything. I fell over some iron bars Richard had set up for cooking and grazed my left shin. Stupid.

2 September – DAY 38

Woke as a massive thunderstorm immediately overhead got into gear. Fortunately it had burned itself out by the time we left. Masha was much more energetic today (Ali is still riding her without a bit), and Pompeii's back is better but he is not quite fit to ride yet, so I rode Muffin, who was in a foul mood and kicked Pompeii.

I had to have a pee behind a bush not far from the road, so Ali held Muffin while I took Pompeii with me. First he got stuck in a tree (one foreleg each side, the tree was too big to smash so I had to back him out of that), then he had a pee while I did, then he trod on my foot.

Cross-country nearly all day, except when we had to cross a

main road. Richard, to our surprise, was not there to meet us, but he turned up eventually, the truck having got stuck (again). Ali's walkie-talkie battery died and the spare was a dud, so we have no communication with each other from now on.

We met a lovely grey gelding in one village, but unfortunately he was loose and he really wanted to get to Pompeii. Ali and Muffin got rid of him. Those two have become wonderful herdsmen as this is a problem we frequently have, and it always seems to be the stallion that these loose horses go for.

We also often pass herds of hobbled horses, which we have renamed 'pogo ponies' as they pronk after us. It is surprising how fast they can move, we frequently have to trot quite fast to escape them.

We had a gorgeous short break in the dappled shade of a birch wood situated at the top of a hill. We were all entranced by the wonderful views all round – I still cannot get over the sheer vastness of this country. After the break I rode Masha, and I do admit I had bit of a struggle with two horses both wearing only head-collars.

Our early campsite in an idyllic valley was interrupted by three locals who had come to inspect us. The rider of a very stocky horse was quite attractive in a gypsy way, but Ali was frightened of them all and kept out of the way. I made polite conversation about where I bought the horses, how much I paid for them, how long it would take to get home, and answered their questions. I am not yet in the habit of translating these conversations, which is very rude of me, and Richard had to keep asking what was going on.

I like Richard very much. He is not only very competent but much more fun than I expected, but there is quite a lot of tension between him and Ali.

3 September – DAY 39

Woke as usual before the alarm went off, and said 'Good morning' to Richard. 'It's 4am' he told me, so I went back to sleep. It started raining as I sat by the camp fire drinking tea, and rained on and off until about 11am. We went very well for the first three or four hours and I rode Pompeii for the first time since he got warble-fly damage a few days ago. He was full of beans after such a long time off.

We had to cross the railway line, the Orel by-pass and then we had to ride up the main Kursk-Orel road for about seventeen kilometres (ten miles). Fortunately there was very little traffic, and there were wide verges and stubble fields for most of the way, so we continued to make good time.

Pompeii went lame at the trot on the near-fore in the middle of Krome. We caused quite a stir in the marketplace by waiting for Richard (who was doing some shopping), and when a tipsy man came up and started talking to me, we remembered an urgent appointment elsewhere, which meant we had to continue to ride up the main road until Richard found us.

I decided to get off and lead Pompeii for the last hundred yards to our second pit stop, and we were (yet again) hailed by Kalashnikov-toting policemen wearing flak-jackets. All the usual questions ('Who are you?' 'Where do you come from?' 'Do you have documents?' 'Where are you going?') with all the usual answers followed by the inevitable 'Why?' (flattering answer – 'Because our horses are so spoilt and yours are so strong'). They then found Richard and they were actually looking at the documents when we caught up – the first officials to do so since I set out.

Ali diagnosed Pompeii as having tendon damage, we guessed the damage was done when we rode across a field which we thought was just a meadow, only to discover it had been ploughed (probably a couple of years before) and left to the grasses, weeds and herbs. We couldn't stop where we were, so we applied cooling gel (during which he nearly smashed my right cheek-bone with his knee) and I changed to Masha and led him the remaining eight kilometres (five miles) to the most perfect camp-site – a birch wood giving dappled shade, high on the hill, blessed by a lovely breeze, with masses of excellent grass and no burrs. Burrs and teazles have been the bane of our lives. Wherever there is long, luscious grass, there are burrs which wind themselves into the horses' manes and tails. The larger ones, about the size of a small ping-pong ball, are very fuzzy and each one has to be individually pulled out. The small ones, about the size of peas, seem to drop out naturally after a day or so.

Richard is worried because I think I am losing weight and I stupidly asked him what the condensed milk situation was. Now I shall have to pretend I am gaining weight to reassure him. My waist-chain, trousers and bum-bag are all far too loose, though.

The food is excellent, thanks to Ali, though why I should be losing weight and feeling so tired is a mystery.

I am still very cheerful, although Pompeii's lameness is a real bugger. Let's hope he is a really tough Russian horse and recovers quickly.

The horses' characters are beginning to emerge. Pompeii is still the rather dreamy stallion I fell in love with last year while Malishka (Muffin) is extremely knowing and very much aware of everything going on around her. She is also a dreadful coward. Masha has the typical Russian pessimistic attitude to everything, and ought really to be rechristened Eeyore.

4 September – DAY 40
After deciding to take a rest day, we certainly had a quiet day. Richard and I left Ali, with the translating machine and some misgivings, and went to the village, Aplkovo, and asked for a farrier. We were told that yes, there was a pensioner called Ivan Ileevitch. We found him eventually in his garden, but it turned out that his father had been a farrier and Ivan used to help him. He and his wife were absolutely charming, chattered on about how there were no more farriers because there were no horse-shoes nowadays, asked where we were going and all the usual questions. What connection can there be between the collapse of communism and the lack of horse-shoes? Or is it the other way around – what connection is there between the rise of communism and a dearth of horse-shoes?

After insisting we take some apples, they let us go, telling me that their children all lived in the town and spat upon village life (until they wanted potatoes or apples). We had already noticed that in Russia, like in many parts of England, most villages seem populated almost entirely by the over-fifties.

We returned to find Ali unmolested (it does worry me, leaving someone so beautiful alone in this rather wild country). We had a drink and some lunch, and I dozed, waking only to take my washing off the line when rain started spitting.

Pompeii's leg is much better. He is not lame, even when going downhill to drink from the stream, and there is no heat and no swelling. We all hope this improvement is maintained as we must press on tomorrow. I do love that little horse, even when he practically breaks my cheek-bone – he is such a character. Ali found him standing motionless today, looking rather surprised. He had wrapped his tether round a tree and couldn't graze!

5 September – DAY 41

We set off with high hopes, and Pompeii seemed completely sound. He travelled well, gradually trotting more and more often. Went across country all day, including through some seriously remote villages, which were so quiet that even the tracks were still grassy. Richard got stuck in one of these when the nearside front wheel had slipped off a bridge. To me it looked terminal, but he managed to jack it up and get the wheel on to a plank and get himself out of it. Meanwhile a very old, deaf man was helping, not put out one whit by the fact that Richard obviously could not understand a single word he was saying.

Soon after that Ali and I were pulled over by the local police. I showed them my passport (Ali's was in the truck) and explained that all the documents for the horses were in our car. The policemen set off in hot pursuit, but when Richard returned half an hour later he said he had not seen them.

Incidentally, it seems that over the last two or three days the local accent is noticeably less thick, and also that an increasing number of gardens have flowers as well as vegetables.

We had a short rest at 11.30am, and again at 3.30pm (when we had to move the horses as soon as we had tethered them because a local babushka came up and begged us to go elsewhere – it was the only patch where she could tether her cow) after which Pompeii was lame again. God knows what went wrong. We could not stop where we were, so we continued for about another eight kilometres (five miles) to another lovely camp site on the edge of a wood. As we rode, Pompeii became less lame, which was encouraging. We did about fifty kilometres in all, which was not bad. I just pray that little stallion is OK tomorrow and that we don't do any permanent damage to his tendon.

6 September – DAY 42

Up at 5.15am as usual, though tired. Before checking if Pompeii was sound, we spent quite a lot of time discussing what to do if he wasn't, like asking the British Embassy in Minsk if they could find some stables near that city to which he could be sent to rest

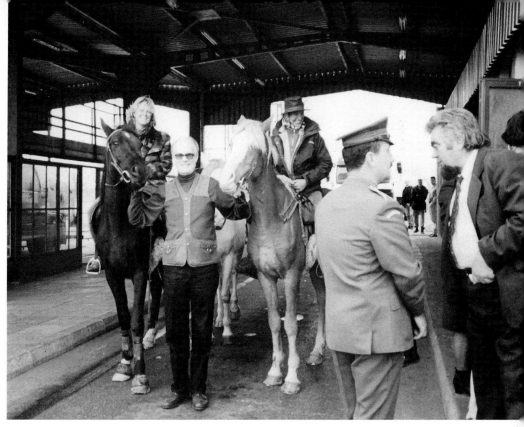

Giles is extremely pleased to see us after four months. Crossing the
Belarus–Poland border

Mealtime at Marek's
gorgeous house in
Kuligi, Poland

Crossing the bridge in Malbork (originally Marienbad) in Poland

Running repairs in Poland

Above: Josef shows Katie and me his stud's collection of carts in Bialy Bor, Poland

Right: Katie and Richard try to get warm – Poland

Katie giving the horses a drink – Poland

Eastern Poland – Poland was so beautiful we all wanted to stay forever

The moment it all ended – the last dismount

The horses had never heard a champagne cork and never seen a flash-bulb, so all recoiled in horror. (© Jonathan Buckmaster/*Daily Express*)

Above: Getting acquainted with Pompeii and Masha's first-born, Ashibka.
(© John Downing/*Daily Express*)

Left: Masha with one-week-old Ashibka. (© John Downing/*Daily Express*)

Pompeii and I at home in Denston: the first quiet moment for six months

Pompeii and I share a joke in May 1996

Ashibka the foal in May 1996

until we caught up. As it turned out, he was sound and, because we didn't trot all day and only did about thirty kilometres, he stayed sound all day. Hope springs eternal. . . .

We really enjoyed our riding today. We spent virtually all day going across country on tracks with only three delays. The first was when the Toyota crashed through an iffy wooden bridge and had to be jacked up, which took about one and a half hours. We then took the horses across, which Richard filmed. It was quite a dangerous bridge. Apart from the fact that many of the timbers were rotten, there were also a lot of rusty nails sticking up out of the planks and it goes without saying that there was no parapet.

We then agreed to meet Richard at a certain point because, although we could cross the next river, he couldn't. What none of us had realized was that beyond the river was a huge marsh area which we had to skirt round. We might have crashed across (but I doubt it) had it not been for my paranoia about Pompeii's tendon, so we lost another half an hour or so there.

The final delay was a delightful one. We stopped at a village shop where Richard had bought bread, vodka and fruit juices without my help. When I came on the scene I asked about buying oats and the charming young couple, who were expecting their first baby, said they had some at home. We went to her mother's house, where they were living while waiting for the baby.

While the oats were loaded, we were invited to lunch and delicious soup, liver, bread, milk, cheese, cucumbers and honey were pressed upon us. I was plied with questions, and am getting better about remembering to translate, so was even slower than usual about finishing my food.

They told us that in June 1986 they went to Kiev and were perplexed by everything in the countryside being black and burned – they had not been told about Chernobyl which happened in April. In this area they were affected, but patchily.

In the meantime, all the men of the village had come to inspect the horses (we had tied Pompeii to a tree and left the mares to wander), and one rather drunk young man rubbished Muffin and Pompeii, but really fancied Masha and offered to exchange her for one of his. I laughingly said no, but he was most persistent. In the end I said it was quite impossible and that apart from liking her, I had all the necessary documents to take her across the borders.

We followed their directions, and crossed the road which took us into Bryansk county (another milestone).

As we rode, Ali and I discussed my future. She thinks I would be mad not to use my Russian somehow, and suggested I take an exam, such as an A level, to find out how I 'match up to the competition'. I said I need urgently to build up my vocabulary and grammar, which I could probably do by reading. I also had the thought that it would be very good for me if I were to spend say, six months in Moscow, if I can get a job there and live with a family where nobody speaks English. Ali suggested I contact the British Embassy there to see if they have any jobs going. I could also ask Sasha.

Back in the real world, Richard found an even more wonderful than usual campsite in a hidden valley surrounded by woods. Incidentally, the charming family had told us that there were no bears here, only wolves.

In the evening, a man and a boy suddenly appeared in our camp. I grabbed Pompeii which was just as well as the man was riding a stallion. They made brief conversation (they were a bit odd, maybe the man was drunk), before moving on. The boy, who looked about ten years old, but must have been older as he was openly smoking, asked about our saddles, and then asked why we did not go bareback, a question we had also been asked at our previous stop. There is only one answer – after six to eight hours it is not comfortable.

CHAPTER SEVEN

Bryansk – County of Forests and Wolves

(and ticks and mosquitoes)

7 September – DAY 43
My alarm dragged me from deep slumber. Richard was still
asleep so I fed the horses, whereupon he woke up. Pompeii is so
greedy and neighs so loudly as soon as he sees somebody moving in the camp that he has become everybody's alarm clock.
Foul day (there have to be some, I just hope there are not too
many); it started raining at about 5.30am and has not stopped
since. Richard had problems with the Toyota but only when trying to drive up hills. We went well, but slowly (I am still leading
Pompeii, and we are still not trotting), and covered forty-three
kilometres. The last sixteen kilometres were abysmal. It was still
raining, and we were crossing the dreariest plain on the planet
with only hideous buildings in view. The only good thing about
the afternoon was seeing the school bus – a horse-drawn cart
driven by a stunningly good-looking man. Richard has found an
OK campsite very near the main road, but hidden from sight. We
are soaking, the horses are soaking, the tack and all our clothes
are soaking – but the awning is up, the fire is blazing and Ali has
just announced supper.

8 September – DAY 44
An even fouler day. It poured with rain all night, I slept badly,
and we set off on the horses in a downpour. The sun appeared
magically once, then downpour followed a dryish patch over
and over again. We did about twenty-four kilometres, on and
beside roads, then off for about eight kilometres on a beautiful
forest path before we found Richard and truck, which had bellied

out. We waited for two hours before he got the truck out with Ali's help, only for one wheel to sink immediately into a rut. It was then decided that we should go ahead on the horses. Within a few hundred yards, however, the track became a swamp, so we returned to Richard. We are now at an awful campsite in a tiny clearing in the middle of the forest, with no grazing for the horses, and it is still raining.

The houses here in the county of forests are made of wood, which is much nicer than the earlier brick ones – but they are still the same tiny size. The people continue to be as friendly as ever.

There seem to be three ways of getting water – from a pump, from a well or via a pulley arrangement which looks exactly like the ancient siege catapults. We found one being worked today, creaking up and down, so of course the horses freaked out.

Pompeii after two trots became lame again (but only at the trot).

9 September – DAY 45

Woke with an enormous weight on my head – the awning was full of water and it was all on top of my bivvy-bag. Baled it out (about three or four bucketfuls), then fed the horses. We shall have to watch Pompeii – he is always a thug but I think he tried to bite me this morning in his eagerness. Poor buggers, they have been out in driving rain all night, with short tethers because there are dangerous holes and treacherous sand here. Luckily they ate very well while Richard was digging himself out yesterday.

It stopped raining as we set off, and didn't rain again all day, which was absolute heaven. We retraced our steps for a couple of miles, and then found another, much better, track. There were some very deep puddles but we managed: Ali led Pompeii for the first time because I was on Muffin who had kicked him a couple of days ago.

A strange insect landed on me – usually I don't mind but somehow this one looked rather sinister, so I brushed it off. It landed on Muffin, so with some difficulty, I brushed it off her.

We crossed a really beautiful small river on a slightly iffy wooden bridge (I had to lead Pompeii over first). Then followed a track raised high over some beautiful marshes and swamps.

The real horror was next: the bridge over the beautiful huge river was a series of old tree trunks, some of them rotten and with some quite large gaps between them, laid across some rusty floating pontoons. Even Pompeii, sensing my fear, was reluctant to take the first step down, but in the end he angelically led his mares across (Ali riding the ever-resigned Masha and leading the cowardly Muffin). He was uneasy, though, and as soon as he realized we were more than half-way over, he tried to rush, pushing me towards the edge (there was no parapet). I managed to calm him and soon we were all safely over, breathing huge sighs of relief. Thinking about it this evening, it occurs to me that we were actually lucky that it has rained so much in the last few days: it must have brought the level of the river up quite significantly. Had we arrived a week or so earlier I am sure there would have been a much steeper angle to the bridge.

We did road work for the rest of the day, through an industrial estate, then trawled slowly along the main street of what must be Russia's longest village, and under a railway bridge. It was a boring trek along a dreary road but we were happy because it wasn't raining!

Found another sinister insect again on Masha, and asked Ali what it was – a tick. Yuck! Lev picked one up weeks ago, but I didn't think they were a real problem.

10 September – DAY 46

Up at 3.30am for a pee when Pompeii saw me and shouted loudly because he thought it was time for his breakfast, and woke everyone. At breakfast Ali moaned that she could not sleep properly, she was cold, the mattress kept deflating, and that something had to be done. Richard told her to 'stop whingeing' whereupon she turned her full fury on him and told him at great length not to be so 'fucking patronising' and so on, while I heartily wished I was somewhere else.

A good day to start with, first on roads (boring), then across country. We came upon our first fence of the trip, so had to go round it. We were then faced with a river and a swamp either side, in the middle of nowhere, and with only one boarded-up empty house to be seen. How could we cross to the other side, where we were to meet Richard? Whom should we ask? I heard music and we found another house and went there. As Ali said, we must have seemed like creatures from another planet as we rode into their yard. 'Can we get to the other side?' I asked.

Babushka swung into operation. 'No, it is not possible, you must follow the road to the bridge', then added more convoluted instructions. We decided they were the Russian equivalent of the Addams family: Babushka was very much in charge, her husband appeared to be mute. There was a good-looking son (he could not have been her son-in-law because no fine male like that would have married into that family), his cowering wife and their two-year-old baby, and a really mean-looking woman in her forties, whom we decided afterwards was probably a daughter. There were no neighbours for literally miles. This was unique in my experience and I had come to assume that Russians always live in communities.

We followed the track, and found Richard and the bridge at the same time. We had been dreading the bridge, but it turned out to be a solid, concrete structure. Why is it that the big roads crossing Russia's finest rivers so often have the most appallingly dangerous bridges, while tiny farm tracks are given decent solid ones?

We stopped for a brief graze, and ever since then Pompeii has been driven mad by an itchy nose, so I suppose he must have encountered some stinging nettles. He smashed my leg so many times, trying to rub it on me or Masha, that eventually Ali put a lead rope on the other side and we frog-marched him along, not allowing him to come near either of us. Poor bugger. When we made camp he just rolled and rolled, and lunged for ages until Richard fed him and then Ali went and talked to him, and knocked him on the forehead gently which seemed to hypnotise him.

Tomorrow is to be a rest day when we find another site, preferably with water and firewood, and without mosquitoes.

11 September – DAY 47

We set off soon after 8am, and rode out of camp. I was on Pompeii because I couldn't cope with his rubbing and anyway, even after lunging for ages last night his tendon was fine this morning. After about three miles we came across Thomas, the Toyota Truck, which was stuck again. While Richard struggled to get free, Ali and I rode on for about half a mile on a hideously muddy track through a beautiful forest, hoping either to get to the other side or to find another road so that Richard could drive round and meet us. Unfortunately we failed.

We staked out the horses, then I returned to help Richard. The rear differential was a problem – the ground clearance is inadequate for the conditions out here – but after four hours we got it out, and I have now learned a great deal about how to get out of mud. In the meantime Ali, bless her, was cleaning the tack, a job we seldom have time for.

Having freed the truck, Richard and I returned to the campsite. It was surrounded by forest, and there was excellent grazing, but unfortunately we were plagued by mosquitoes. These are now very active in the warmth after all the rain we have had, which has left bogs and stagnant puddles everywhere. In fact, I have christened this campsite 'The joint is jumping' because, apart from mosquitoes, there are grasshoppers and frogs galore, as well as the usual ladybirds which are taking on plague proportions. Pompeii is not happy at all, but he is grazing and not as hysterical as yesterday except for the odd bit of circling (always on the right leg).

Richard went off to inspect a second track, which he thought might be passable. While he was away, Ali washed and I took my dress off to let the air at my body. Inspecting myself casually, I found on my bottom what I thought was a wild oat seed or similar (of which I still have to pick about 300 off my jodhpurs), but I couldn't get rid of it. Horrors, was it a tick? I shrieked at Ali and asked her to look at it. It was a tick, and – bless her – she eventually burnt it off with a cigarette, which was quite painful but far better than leaving it in. I am now completely neurotic if any poor innocent insect lands on me.

Richard returned and got the awning up just before the rain started. We relaxed and enjoyed the evening. Ali cooked as usual, we watered the horses and moved their tethering stakes (none of us had realized Pompeii had circled so much he had wrapped his rope round the stake and only had about four feet of grazing circle). After supper I read again through the diary Giles had kept (for the first time in his life) to keep me up to date with home and village life, in the hope that I shall feel less like a total stranger when I get back. Why am I not homesick?

12 September – DAY 48

We set off with me riding Pompeii and Ali on Masha along the second track. We soon realized that Richard would never be able to follow, but our parting words had been that if he could not get through he would go round by road and meet us at Klyetnya, and I said 'by the railway' because we knew from the map that there was one.

It was eerie splashing through a misty forest, not sure where we were going but using the compass frequently. In a clearing we surprised four or five wild boar, which was a real delight. After about two hours of complete silence and solitude we heard a dog bark and went towards it, followed by a loose horse that had come to inspect us. I asked the way to Klyetnya and was told to follow the road (an excellent wide, sandy track), and that it was about twenty kilometres.

The road took us to a village, where I checked the way with a woman and was told to turn right along the road, there was another cross-country route but there wasn't too much traffic on the road. We followed the road that gradually became a track, then a path, and led us through bogs until it became a track and then a road – not once did we see a car – which led us to the tarmac road. We wondered what the cross-country track would have been like. The first car we saw was a German-registered Mercedes. Then we were in Klyetnya, and it was still only noon. Ali and I have decided that the way the tracks peter out between villages is as if the locals set out towards the next village and then just give up and go home again.

In Klyetnya we found the station. No Richard. I asked two people if there was a level crossing and was told 'nyet'. We waited, getting increasingly worried, for four hours. Fortunately there was masses of excellent grazing outside the station. In what other country would grass be provided in the middle of town?

We attracted a lot of attention, particularly among the children. When they found out we were English they wanted to know why I was speaking Russian. I said I had thought they probably would not be able to speak English so I had learned their language. 'Was I right? Can you speak English?' 'Of course, we can't speak English'. 'So it is just as well I learned Russian then, isn't it?' I still have some linguistic problems. These people have never met foreigners, so when I say I don't understand a word they just keep repeating it, the concept of selecting a synonym is quite alien to them. This is normal even among the grown-ups, and I now realize I was extraordinarily lucky to be staying with a woman as intelligent and sensitive as Tatiana.

At 4pm, by which time I was convinced Richard was dead or dying, we went to the police. I explained our problem and our concerns to the Russian equivalent of the duty sergeant. 'We can't do anything,' he mumbled. 'Then what should I do?' I asked. Eventually a more senior man appeared and I explained the situation all over again. I certainly had to lay on the charm in a big way, helpless foreign woman appealing to this big, strong Russian man for help. Anyway, it worked even though he was horrified that my visa was only for Moscow. ('In London they think Moscow is everywhere' I told him, and he laughed.)

Suddenly Richard appeared. He had got stuck and had been waiting for hours at the level crossing that I had been told did not exist.

We then had more problems because we had not registered, so I repeated the old line that my friends at the Academy of Science had assured me it was not necessary.

After two hours, umpteen phone calls and a complicated form for each of us, we were allowed to go. The form, incidentally, demanded to know what we did and how much we earned. I said it varied. He said, 'Well, on average?' I thought quickly and said about US $120 (£80). 'A month?' Oh Christ, I can't say – 'No, a day' so I told him it was 'per week'. 'You earn much more than we do, I only get US $100 (£66) a month'. 'Yes I know, but our things are much more expensive, especially vodka', which got another laugh.

As we rode out of town, Ali said that while I was doing battle in the police station Richard had been so rude to her she had almost burst into tears. I can see exactly what is happening here. Ali is a Virgo to the extent that she can't keep quiet. She obviously implied (and not for the first time) that Richard had made a mistake, first by getting stuck and then by not finding us in a small town. Richard does not like to be criticized. I made noises and said there was nothing I could do: she has indicated she might bail out when we get to Poland. What a mess. I certainly can't leave them alone together again.

We are now in the lovely secluded campsite where Richard found two Camberwell Beauty butterflies on a log. We have seen the first signs of fencing (albeit in a terrible state of collapse) since the one near the Russian Addams family. These fences form what must have been cattle corrals in the forest clearings.

CHAPTER EIGHT

Smolensk County

12 September – DAY 49

Thinking about Richard v Ali, I am in a quandary. I have always liked Ali enormously, but I like Richard too, although he can be a little spiky, and he probably should not have tried to get through the forest tracks yesterday.

I must talk to Giles and see if he can find another bod or two for Germany, as I am already feeling uneasy about Germany after my experience ten years ago, when I took a friend's camper van and drove round France, Belgium, Luxembourg and Germany with Katie (then aged about fourteen). In the first three countries we had simply parked wherever we wanted in the evenings, had a meal and gone to sleep. On our first night in Germany we did the same, but were soon surrounded by about twenty young men on their motorbikes. They were so menacing that I decided discretion was the better part of valour, especially as Katie was so young, and we drove to the nearest hotel.

We mounted up and all went well for about twenty kilometres (twelve miles). Half-way through a village, a lorry driver stopped and called to Ali. When I came along to translate, I eventually understood that he and his mate wanted us to get in the back of the lorry (it was like a skip or dumper-truck) and drink vodka with them (it was 9am). I laughingly declined on the grounds that we had to hurry to England.

On the outskirts of Semirichi we were halted by our first encounter with a road block. The officials were charming, but told us that some horses had recently been stolen, so we had to wait for two and a half hours while they radioed Klyetnya with the details on the horse passports (showing where I had

purchased them). The police there would presumably then contact the police in Alexikovo who (Vassily Vadianov not having a
telephone) probably had to go out to his farm to check with him
and then the information would have to be relayed back, and so
on. We used the time to graze the horses and have a snack ourselves.

In spite of that delay we have done fifty-six kilometres today.

In Korsiki (first village in Smolensk region) we were hailed by
a very pleasant barefoot woman in her fifties or sixties. She
wanted to know all about us, then started searching in my sad-
dlebag, rather to my surprise. It turned out she was looking for
my gun. She then dragged us over to meet the rest of the family,
all (including her) having obviously had a boozy lunch. She
begged us to join them for a meal, but I excused ourselves on the
grounds that Richard was waiting for us and would be worried.
I had a chat with a young blond man with a moustache, who was
probably her grandson, and was fascinated by our journey.

At about 4pm we met a thunderstorm. These Russian ones
have a character all of their own. The clouds blow in a different
direction from the rain, and the lightning, literally around you, is
followed by a thunderclap immediately overhead – four seconds
later. We couldn't have got wetter had we been swimming.

There is a really nice atmosphere in this region. We rode
through a fabulously beautiful birch wood after leaving the road
block. Now, and for the last few days, not only are there flowers
in the gardens but geraniums in windows. There are also very
few tethered animals in the villages as they are all picketed out
on the outskirts. We have seen a lot of wild lupins over the last
ten days or so.

I am still enquiring about a farrier, with still no luck.

Four or five days ago, while riding across a gloomy plain,
we saw people picking widely-spaced flowers. Ali looked and
realized it was opium poppy! Out here it is probably used medi-
cinally – if my grasp of the language were better I would love to
ask these country folk what ancient remedies they use to treat ill-
nesses in humans and livestock.

We left at 7.45am and did well. After a break at about 11am we
were just tacking up again when a passing tractor screeched to a
halt. Out jumped a man and a woman who rushed over to
Richard (it still makes me laugh that everyone always assumes
that, being the only man, he is the only one that counts). When

they realized that I was the only one they could communicate with, they asked if we needed oats, which we did. We are all stunned – here was a Russian with the initiative to see the horses with a car and instantly make the connection that horses need oats. They wanted to know if we were gypsies, and when we denied it, they then accused us of being tourists.

Our next encounter was with a gang of women who were very surprised that we were women. 'No man!' they exclaimed. '*Ni nada*' ('We don't need one') I answered. Thirty seconds' silence was followed by roars of laughter. We met up with Richard by a level crossing, and he gave us Kendal Mint Cake and filled our water bottle before going into Roslav to phone Giles or Sasha. Incidentally, I think I now understand why Russian trains go so slowly: only in towns do the level crossings have gates (where they are always manned). On country roads, car drivers (and horse riders) just have to stop and look before crossing the railway.

At this stop, at my request, Richard also gave us the horse passports, which was just as well as we were stopped twice by the police. The first lot were in an ordinary Lada, and as usual Ali and I both thought we were being attacked as the car screeched to a halt in front of us and two blokes (in plain clothes) leapt out of the car. The second policeman who stopped us was on a motorbike.

We plodded on, through Shumiachi and on to Dubovnitsa. There are many roads in Shumiachi so I had to ask the way. Our map of Russia was printed in Poland, and I cannot understand the Polish spelling, so I had some problems with pronunciation.

CHAPTER NINE

Belarus

15 September – DAY 51

I'm in my bivvy-bag now. It is miserably cold, with a howling wind and drenching rain, and I feel so sorry for the poor horses, who are staked out. We have made it to Belarus, though. We forded the river border but it was too deep for the Toyota, so Ali and I had to wait in driving rain for an hour while Richard went round.

This morning we met a really nice *sympatichnye* (roughly translating as kind and friendly) shepherd on the road (only the second or third country person we have seen wearing glasses) who, when hearing about us, first accused us of being tourists and then asked how I had learned Russian. I told him from tapes. 'Do you have Russian lessons in England?' I said we did, but that I was too old. Immediately after leaving him we found a puppy whining, cold, miserable and soaking wet at a bus stop: of course we now have it (with the shepherd's blessing!)

Exhausted.

16 September – DAY 52

What a contrast. After a miserable night when the storm continued unabated, we got up and pulled on our soaking wet clothes and put wet saddles on the saturated horses, who were literally shivering. We rode into Mstislavl, where I saw a man driving a horse whose feet clip-clopped! I rushed over and asked him where I could find a farrier, to be told there was one at Konyezavod.

The people here seem rather guarded at first, but pride

certainly exists and we are very obviously in a different country. This is a nice town, with plenty of shops – apparently we can even telephone England – and we are surrounded by tidy houses and gardens. Quite a culture shock.

On and on through the town, near the centre of which we found Richard talking to a crowd of very welcoming and pleasant policemen. I interpreted their conversation – Richard wanted to know where he could change money as it is Saturday. My Belarus visa is now hopelessly out of date, and I don't fancy a spell in prison here, so I asked the policemen what to do. They had no idea. Thanks, boys. They were all very interested in our journey, and (as we stood there shivering in the icy rain) suggested we go to a hotel. I said fine, did the hotel also take horses? They told us there were excellent stables at Konyezavod, which I realized was not a village but actually means horse factory (stud). Soaked to the skin, I mounted up again and, after getting lost once, we finally arrived.

The usual pantomime ensued. 'I am English, we are riding to England'. 'Can you keep our horses until Monday morning?'. 'Can you put one shoe each on the stallion and the black mare – I have my own horse-shoes.' Eventually all was fixed, and my horses were led away to God knows what, but it will be no worse than what they are used to and a lot better than last night.

The kind director of the stud drove Ali and me to the hotel (such a difference from the snooty director of the place where I left Rada in Lisky). Wonder of wonders, our room has a loo. It also offers a hot and a cold tap, but unfortunately the hot one doesn't work.

We had lunch at an adjoining restaurant where, out of a huge menu, valid from 15 – 17 September, the waitress ticked three things. We thought that she was indicating the dishes which were not available, but we are close enough to Russia for it to mean the things that were available.

Richard and Ali went shopping while I dozed. Then off to the public *Bannia* where the assistant, Lyuba, on finding out we were English was overcome with delight, took us in hand, and even stripped off herself to beat us with birch twigs. I heard her telling all the other women about our trip, and when we had finished she insisted we first have 'water' (oversweet fruit juice), then vodka, then a biscuit.

She was so warm and friendly that we have invited her to

supper at the hotel, and are waiting for her now. She said she would be here on the dot of 8pm, which I don't believe because that's when she stops work.

Meantime, the puppy, named by me *Ashibka* (mistake) continues to enchant. She is amazingly quick to learn and eats porridge or leftovers though she is riddled with fleas, and we shan't be able to find a vet tomorrow (Sunday).

17 September – DAY 53
Lyuba not having turned up by 8.30pm, I went down to join Richard. Ali appeared fifteen minutes later and we ordered food and a bottle of wine. I went to inspect the wine (there were three types on the menu, all claiming to be dry, but the first on the list was Muscat, so I was a bit dubious). I was shown a bottle with a Hungarian label so I accepted it. It appeared that it was not just the only type of wine available, but the only bottle. When the waitress brought it to the table, she also brought the corkscrew because she didn't know how to use it.

The restaurant was full of young men, one of whom was very pissed and wobbled over to our table. I asked him where all the girls were, and in answer he pointed to the 'House of Culture' opposite and told me there was a disco in there. Very cultured.

At 9.10pm Lyuba turned up, so we hastily added her order to ours. Within a very short time she was extremely drunk which, of course, having a Russian soul, even if this is Belarus, meant she was inconsolably sad and spent the rest of the evening crying her eyes out. With some difficulty, Ali and I got her into the car and drove her home.

I slept very badly in the first bed I have been in since we left Nikolai and Tatiana's, and finally got up at about 8.30am with a headache. I had quite a bit of vodka last night but not that much, so I think quality must have been very poor. Ashibka had had a crap (which I trod in, fortunately after putting my shoes on) and a couple of piddles, so I took her outside.

Back and neck are very stiff from the earlier struggles with Pompeii (if we are on the verge he tries to trot on the tarmac) and struggles yesterday with Masha, who put the brakes on when I was leading them to the stables. I chose to walk the last mile or two because I thought it might warm me up a fraction, and it did. I actually started off in the morning on foot, but Pompeii was so miserable and het up by the icy wind he tried to rear and was generally so much trouble I had to mount Masha after about a mile.

Later

Went to phone Giles but didn't have enough money. Richard still being conspicuous by his absence, Ali and I raided the truck and found US $20 (£13). Rang Giles, he was very happy to hear from me because he had decided 'since you didn't ring last time but sent Richard, I was sure something had happened to you.'

Tried to ring Nina Pavlovna in Moscow, but there was no reply. The very friendly woman at the post office suggested I try again in a couple of hours' time, and, in the course of our conversation, I discovered that Belarus is one hour behind Moscow, which explains why Lyuba was so late last night.

Ali and I went and bought bread, cheese and mandarin juice, which we consumed while waiting for Giles's call. By noon we were so worried about Richard, we knocked really loudly, whereupon he emerged with a bit of a hangover. Ali and I had lunch (he couldn't face it), then rested while he took the Toyota to the stables and dried everything out. Weather dry and sunny but there is an icy wind. He saw the horses, and reported that everything seemed fine, but that the horses had not been shod.

Ali and I went shopping, first to a book shop where I bought what I thought was a Russian fairy story – only when I looked closely later did I find it was written by Tolkien! The woman in the shop was very friendly and interested, and explained the difference between Belarus and Russian spelling ('i' instead of 'u', etc.).

I spent two hours trying to translate the instructions for geiger-counter, which was extremely frustrating as I had to look up almost every word and the result was still meaningless. I have decided to ask somebody to read it and tell me which bits matter. Meanwhile Ali and Richard went to the *Bannia*, but Lyuba was not there – we hope she hasn't lost her job.

People here – once the ice is broken – seem very warm and, on the whole, more forthcoming than in Russia. In the restaurant, a garish blonde addressed me in German. Later she called me over, giving me the chance to explain we were English, and she urged us to go to the disco. I said that nothing would give me more pleasure, but that we were very tired.

18 September – DAY 54
Slept badly again. We emerged from the hotel to find quite a sharp frost, the first of the winter, I was told later.

We left at 7.30am, and arrived at Konyezavod ten minutes later (so twenty minutes earlier than our expected time of 8am). The director was busy and sent one of his men to show us round the stud. They breed heavy horses – Ardennes. They were magnificent, and the stables were by far the cleanest and best run I have ever seen in Russia (but this is Belarus). My three (in a cowshed) were finishing their oats, and were then given some freshly wilted hay. They have all lost weight after that awful night in the storm.

We then waited around for two hours. As usual, we had no idea why but I didn't mind because the horses were eating. Eventually they were brought to be shod. The farrier rushed over to tell me that Muffin was in foal (how did he know? I didn't dare ask because I would never have understood the answer) and that she should be kept under cover. Impossible until we get to England, I told him. He shrugged.

Then to the director's office to pay and leave, but of course he was out. The chap on duty called him on the radio and he promised to return in twenty minutes. We decided to tack up the horses, but on returning to the stables, found they had been given yet another bucket of oats. Everyone groaned except me, and Richard said, 'You'll be taking out Russian citizenship soon.'

While we waited, we chatted to the two lads there: listened to the usual complaints of how poor they were, how their wages bought bread and cigarettes only. I know this is true. As usual, I was asked how our life differed. I admitted we were much better paid, but pointed out that, for example, a new English saddle cost at least US $750 (£500), which made them think, 'We can buy a car for that here'. 'Exactly', I replied.

Back to the director's office, where to my horror, after presenting me with a badge of his stud, he refused to accept any payment, saying we had been their guests. After thanking him profusely and feeling very embarrassed, we left. Unfortunately, the road he told us to take turned out to be the wrong one, but never mind.

Incidentally, I offered Ashibka to the office staff, as I offer her to everyone we meet, because I could not face putting her into quarantine, never mind facing the cost.

We did well over twenty-nine kilometres, which was pretty good considering that we didn't start until nearly 1pm. Richard found a lovely campsite, where we witnessed the most amazing sunset.

19 September – DAY 55

Ashibka shared my sleeping bag for most of the night, and she makes quite a good self-heating hot-water bottle. Fortunately she has (so far) had the manners to keep her fleas to herself. The night was bitterly cold, but anything is better than the driving rain.

We were in the saddle at 7am, and we covered fifty-eight kilometres. We could have done a few more, but my bladder (the cold weather?) has gone into overdrive and I had to stop four times before noon.

The Belarussian people on the whole (by which I mean the ones we do not get the chance to chat to) seem less friendly than the Russians. Pompeii, with the extra ration of oats I asked Richard to give him, is going much better but freaks out at every lorry, especially a new variety, which carries a vast load of what we think are linseed stooks [grouped sheaves of grain], and I must admit they do look fearsome. He was especially badly behaved in Gorki. One lorry going round the corner in Gorki actually had its near-side wheels leave the ground. Ali and I cannot believe we won't soon find one on its back, waving its legs in the air.

Another cold evening, so Richard has lit a campfire. He has found a nice sheltered campsite on the edge of a wood in a huge field full of linseed stooks – each one is individually hand-bound. This cold, at least, makes it unlikely it will rain in the immediate future.

20 September – DAY 56

My alarm went off as usual, and I needed a pee so I got up and fed the horses. It was freezing cold again (-3°C I should think). I only realized when it was too late to go back to bed that it was an hour earlier than intended. I had forgotten yet again to tell the Psion that Belarus was not in the same time-zone as Moscow.

Today we covered about fifty-six kilometres, including through Shlof, quite a big town but we could not avoid it because it contains the only bridge across the river. Pompeii went demented as we crossed the bridge, even though Richard drove the truck behind us to protect our rear, the naughty (or frightened?) stallion went bonkers at every lorry and bus coming towards us or overtaking us. I really thought we would end up going over the parapet, and tried to work out if I could get my feet out of the stirrups before we hit the water.

We have been seeing lots of flax straw, each stook hand-bound. Today we saw a woman working in the fields and trotted over to ask her what it was for. Ali had thought it was used for fuel, but I had said I felt it unlikely because there is a zillion tons of wood readily available. Before I got the answer to my question, I had to answer the woman's questions, but eventually found out that the flax stems go to a local factory to be spun into linen.

We are very worried about the horses: they seem to be losing weight since the awful cold, wet and windy night we crossed the border into Belarus, and the last two freezing nights they have used up all their calories keeping warm because they have not grown their winter coats yet. Pompeii's girth is two holes tighter. At Ali's suggestion, Richard has found a wonderful site in the middle of a forest, but there is nothing to eat. We have given them two-thirds of a bale of HorseHage, the remaining third being kept for the morning, but because the truck only had room for three bales and not the ten I asked for, we are now in trouble.

I have been thinking hard this evening: we must either try and find a building and some hay every night while it is so cold, or camp on the edge of a wood and just bring the horses in when it gets dark. Either way we are going to have to go more slowly. Blast Anna Shubkina – had it not been for the weeks of unnecessary delays we'd be home by now.

21 September – DAY 57
Miraculously slept like a log for nine hours. There was no frost and we were so sheltered I was almost too hot. Indeed, it was cloudy and windy when we emerged from the forest. In one village we found a magnificently-carved well with a bucket thoughtfully attached, so we stopped to water the horses. While we were doing so, a car full of young men screeched to a halt and one of them jumped out to ask which one of us spoke Russian. I

confessed. He wanted to sell me a Trakehner mare. I said sorry, not this time, so he gave me his name and address.

Richard returned and said he would find a good site for our first break within an hours' ride. On and on, out of the village, at a T-junction we turned left (which felt correct, and the compass confirmed it) on to a bigger road. We were stopped by some policemen who were amazed at our journey, did not want to see our documents, asked me why we had a spare horse, and wished us 'bon voyage'.

Over an hour later we started wondering where Richard was, and a radio call revealed we had somehow passed him. He was not pleased, but these things must happen occasionally and it was nobody's fault. Actually it was quite lucky in a way, because where we stopped (after yet more police who insisted on taking notes of everything, including the engine and/or chassis number of the Toyota), we met a very kind man, probably in his sixties. He chatted to us, and offered us the mushrooms he had just picked. We offered him the puppy and he accepted!! He had some coffee and scrambled eggs with us, and then we went back to his house where he gave us some potatoes and beetroot. It has got to be a better home than the bus shelter where we found her, and we were all getting much too fond of her. Incidentally, the new owner gave me his address and I discovered he was two weeks older than I am.

We travelled on in the pouring rain and I was chatted up by yet another policeman (he really was quite attractive, and said he wanted to come with us, so I pointed out we had a spare horse.) We were now on a perfectly hideous main road, but a lot of the time we could weave our way through the forest. Richard found some old barns we might be able to use and one old woman directed us to the foreman's house, where we found a hopelessly drunk man who spent ages trying to decide what to do. After about three-quarters of an hour he went back inside to put his boots on to show us somewhere we could stay, but obviously had another drink and forgot us. We then found another house half a mile or so away, and I asked the inhabitants if we could tether our horses in the adjoining orchard, but they told me they were squatters, so we moved round the corner.

We are now in a clearing in the forest, which is very sheltered. It is raining quite hard, but there is plenty of grass and it is not too cold. The men from the neighbouring house came to offer help and the warmth of their cottage, but we were too cold, tired and hungry to make the effort before supper, and are now just too cold and tired.

Ali was in tears during supper but won't say why. I suspect she just can't handle the climate – it must come especially hard to someone who spent last winter in the Caribbean. I am resigned to being wet, cold and miserable until I get home (except when in my wonderfully warm sleeping bag).

22 September – DAY 58
Off early. Met the friendly neighbours and apologized for not turning up last night. It has been a truly ghastly day, on the main road for most of the way, but we made good time by walking for one kilometre and then trotting the same distance. Pompeii has not been too bad about lorries. The weather was misty but dry for the first two hours. I said to Ali, 'Are you all right this morning? I don't want to pry, but if you want to talk about it. . . .' It turned out she was weeping last night because she was upset by a remark from Richard to the effect that 'Your boyfriend will have a new girlfriend by the time we get back'.

I am now sitting in a good campsite with the horses protected from the wind, but it is still wet. The horses are now on over a bucketful of oats a day. I pointed out to Richard and Ali that we could save at least half a day if we went through the middle of Minsk as it will be a Sunday, and Richard (now named 'slave driver') is very happy with that idea. We had to cross yet another bridge on the edge of town, so I led Pompeii because he is so trusting. He was certainly better than last time in Schlof, but that isn't saying much.

Sitting by our wonderful camp-fire, we were certain we could hear wolves. If so, it was the first time, although we have occasionally seen their footprints. The man who took our puppy said there were plenty of wolves but no bears in this region.

23 September – DAY 59
We woke to a lovely morning, with the waning moon on its back, so we hoped for a fine day. Instead we got fog, unaccountably mixed with a raw, chilly wind. We were hailed by an old woman in a village who wanted to know all about us. She then burst into

tears and told us how terribly hard her life was. We also got
another version of how all the young have fled to the towns. I listen very sympathetically to these tales of woe, but feel so helpless. What can I do or say to help these people?

In another village, two men separately asked where were our
pistols. God knows why. I just answered that we didn't need any.

At lunch two young men appeared and chatted to us. They
told us they had never met foreigners before, so I told them we
were people, just like them. In fact, almost none of the people we
come across have ever met a foreigner, so I feel like an ambassador of the west, which is a fairly awesome responsibility. Those
people who had been abroad, like the man who took Ashibka,
invariably told me they had lived and worked in (presumably
East) Germany.

The weather improved and we got quite hot, which of course
meant a million flies.

We are trying out a new system. Alternately trotting and walking for one kilometre seemed too much, so today we tried lots of
short trots, and we cracked the sixty-five kilometres (forty miles)
at last.

Towards the end of the day, in the penultimate village we
passed through, Richard told me he had asked if we could use
someone's phone, which we could. A very nice pair of middle-
aged brothers, who lived in Minsk and for whom this cottage
served as a *dacha*, listened in fascination to my story. They told
me that there had been a third brother who had gone to live in
America, but that they had lost his address.

Using their phone and their help to get the number, I tried to
ring the stables that the British Ambassador in Minsk had recommended to let them know we hoped to be arriving tomorrow
night, but there was no answer. These kind and warm brothers
told me it was a wonderful place and had lots of grazing. If the
worst comes to the worst we can at least camp there and the
horses can eat.

As we passed through the last village of the day we were overtaken by a horseman so drunk he could barely stay in the saddle.
When he got off (which, like all Russians, he did cowboy-style,
leaving his left foot in the stirrup) he then couldn't get his
foot out of the stirrup. The pony was obviously used to it, and
stood stoically. Ali and I laughed unsympathetically for about
five minutes.

I have noticed a new phenomenon, which is that each house in this area has its own well. It occurs to me that someone (the aristocracy in the last century? The Soviet authorities?) must have spent a fortune, because every village, even the poorest, that we have passed through has several wells and I understand that they cost a lot to sink.

We are in a well-sheltered campsite in the forest, but there has been a very unhappy end to the day. Masha (whom I rode all day to give Pompeii a day off) got tangled in her tether on very uneven ground, panicked and fell over. She has done something awful to her neck (initially I thought she had broken it), and is holding her head to the left. After we got her up, she kept falling over unless we held her up, although she walked freely and was not in pain. Ali and Richard are marvellous, and walked her up and down for a while. Now (9pm) it seems a fraction freer and she can stand up unaided. Richard will check her every hour through the night. I hope to God we can get her to the stables tomorrow, where at least they should be able to find a vet. We may have to fill her with bute [a painkiller for horses]. This episode really brings home the fact that we are vulnerable, but at least we have the Toyota and, in an emergency, Richard could drive me to find a vet.

24 September – DAY 60
Richard and Ali both checked Masha frequently during the night, and in fact they had to walk miles to find her (we had left her untethered). When Richard brought us tea at 4.45am he also gave us the welcome news that Masha had just got down, rolled and got up again.

Realizing that there would not be too many bushes on the motorway or in central Minsk, I forwent my morning drink, just in case!

We were on the move just before 6.30am, which meant that Richard had to use the Toyota headlights to illuminate our way through the forest track, although it was quite light enough to see once we had emerged from the trees. We had done about twenty kilometres (thirteen miles) before our lunch break with Masha moving so freely we even risked a couple of canters with no discernible ill-effect.

The weather in the morning was perfect for the horses – cool and cloudy, which meant no flies, although the sun did peep out while we were tethering them for lunch. We have gone from true summer to real autumn in about eight days.

After about twenty-four kilometres of motorway, we arrived in Minsk. It was very crowded with people (but not lorries) and the horses behaved beautifully, but I hope not to have to go through such a big town again. Giles said our Ambassador there had been doubtful about riding through the city, and he was right – we did cause some lovely traffic jams.

Once we got out of the city we had to endure about another eight kilometres of motorway, then at last we turned off on to a country lane and were able to have a bathroom stop in some trees. We walked with the horses for the last kilometre, and left them with some kindly-seeming chaps at the Olympic stables. My three have been put in the servants' quarters, without even a light. We asked that they be given lots and lots of hay and oats, and left them to it.

Richard had booked us into the neighbouring hotel, but there was no hot water, no restaurant, and no facility for ringing England. I suggested that, if we had to go into Minsk to eat and ring Giles, we might just as well try to find a decent hotel. Richard had unpacked the truck and was not pleased with my idea, and decided to stay there whatever happened.

We squashed into the truck and set off. At Ali's suggestion we stopped at a casino, outside which we had given the horses a ten-minute graze during the afternoon. Imagine the scene – very posh decor, staff immaculate in cocktail clothes. Ali and I walk in dressed in filthy jodhpurs, coats, scarves and hats. The atmosphere of disapproval is tangible. I go for broke: 'Excuse me, but we are English and I wonder if you could help us? We need food and a hotel from which I can telephone England'. Instant thaw, smiles all round, 'You must eat here and we will book you into a good hotel'. By the time Richard appeared (having been parking the truck), we were all the best of friends.

We tried to tidy up in the cloakroom (but without much success, I fear), and were led with great ceremony into the restaurant/disco, where I have never felt quite so under-dressed. Fortunately, we were the only customers. We were well fed and they invited us to choose the music. I was even asked what proportions of gin to tonic Richard and Ali would prefer and at intervals the receptionist from downstairs appeared at my elbow to update me on her quest for a hotel. Eventually one was found at a cost of US $24 (£15) per night per person. To cap it all, when the time came to leave they offered us a driver and car to guide us to the hotel.

We checked in and found ourselves surrounded by immense luxury beyond our wildest dreams – the rooms had a loo and a bath, and a shower. We gave our washing to the *dijornaya* (floor manageress) with grovelling apologies about the state of everything and explanations about our journey.

I couldn't have a bath as there was no more hot water (so we are not quite into civilization yet).

25 September – DAY 61
I had a hot bath and washed my hair. The bath water was full of grass and dead leaves, so let the water out, cleaned the bath, then showered and had another hot bath. Richard rang to say he had arrived and checked in.

After coffee (we were too late for breakfast), we returned to the room and I cleaned out my wash pack (a major job) and the part of my day sack that was full of leaked hand cream (another major job).

Lunch (including 'Veat booyion with huff past') cost US $58.08 (£38) for three. The chips were cold, the rest of the food only so-so, but some delightful music played by a trio of pianist, saxophonist and violinist made up for it. Amazingly I was able to pay with my credit card!

Ali and I then went to the stables because Richard had said the director wanted to see me. My horses were tucking into hay, looking well and relaxed. Saw the director briefly, and although he seemed to be in a meeting, he checked the horses' passports and veterinary documents, and told me they charged US $3 (£2) per horse per day (in roubles), which I promised to pay tomorrow as neither of us had any change. I was asked what we were doing in Minsk, as they thought I should have gone through Gomel. I replied that we had been told it was dangerous in Gomel. Dangerous? After Chernobyl, I explained. They laughed.

On our return to Minsk, Ali and I went to the linen shop where I bought Ali a tablecloth and napkin set (a belated birthday present), she bought some more napkins, and we bought ten metres of wonderfully thick, soft fabric, out of which Ali has offered to make me a dressing gown. Roll on summer.

I know we are no longer in wild places, sadly. Not only was I able to have a real bath and use my credit card in the hotel, but I also encountered some Germans in the lobby.

26 September – DAY 62
After breakfast Ali rang Marek (her friend, the horse-breeder) in Poland to tell him our intended itinerary – he was apparently unwell but sounded charming. From the room I rang the British Ambassador to thank him for finding stables at Ramtaka and to ask if he knew of any at Grodna, which he didn't, but said to ask the stable staff at Ramtaka.

Perhaps this is a good moment to explain the system of shopping in Russia (and, so I found out today, in Belarus). You decide what you want to buy, and goods like cheese are cut and weighed and you are told the price. When all purchases have been made, you then queue at the cash desk and tell the woman there what you have bought and how much it cost. The cashier rings it all up, you pay and are given either one receipt – if all your goods came from the same counter – or several. You then return to the counter(s), and you are given the goods when you hand over the cash slip.

After shopping, we then squeezed into the truck and Richard drove us to the stables at Ramtaka, but the director was out, so we went to tack up. In the stable yard we met a man with two beautiful Trakehner stallions and three mares, one of which was a Hanoverian in foal to a Holstein. I filmed quite a bit, and took his address. While waiting for the director to reappear, we had a picnic lunch, finally leaving at 1.30pm. Pompeii was fighting fit, and Masha went very well, but Muffin had not benefited quite so much from her rest. We had to travel along the dual carriageway, but we were able to escape to the fields or woods quite often and Richard found a reasonable campsite. We are all tired, as usual.

Everything now is much more Westernized, but we still attract attention even in the countryside, because we have a spare horse, and because we are women. For how long will this continue? Ali and I mourn the passing of real Russia, but Richard is thrilled to be able to go into a shop with a good chance of finding something he wants to buy. Wild lupins still grow in abundance, and the ladybirds, which had been a positive pest until the cold weather, have reappeared.

27 September – DAY 63
All these time changes mean it gets dark much earlier, so we must start earlier in the mornings.

It drizzled as we set off on the horses, and got steadily worse. We were able to follow the road loosely at first, only getting on to the tarmac once and for not very long.

Lunch was a shock: we found the truck parked outside a motorway café. The horses were tethered on the verge and we went into the dry, but not very warm, café. Of course the staff thought we were German, so I had to put them right. I had some vodka and we all had coffee, chicken, chips and salad, all excellent. The only nuisance was the noise of drills and power saws as the café is still unfinished.

Off again, with me slightly glowing from vodka. Luckily Ali had taken Muffin in tow, as about an hour later we had to return to the road again. I was trudging along in a cocoon of cold, wet misery when Pompeii freaked out completely at an oncoming, overtaking lorry and tried to fling himself under its wheels. I honestly thought my time had come, but somehow I managed to get him back to the verge in the nick of time.

Seriously frightened, we resolved to do everything possible to stay on tracks or to go across fields. As we are now in marshy country, that is not so easy and we sometimes had to go quite a long way from the road. Luckily we had the walkie-talkie (Richard having recharged the batteries in the hotel) and, after a long time away from the road, we were able to contact Richard who had been understandably concerned.

Around late afternoon we stopped to give the horses ten minutes' grazing on some delicious grass. The forest loomed ahead, and Richard came back to tell us that we would have to stay on the road for quite a while. I thought there must be tracks through the forest and Ali agreed, pointing out that the road was hellishly dangerous even for the mares, with lorries hurtling past inches away.

We set off and, to cut a long story short, every track was determined to lead us in any direction except that in which we wished to go. After speaking to Richard on the radio, we tried to head back to the road, but the tracks mulishly refused to let us. We even tried to cut through a clearing but were turned back by a marsh.

I was becoming quite concerned because it was getting dark. I supposed we could survive a night out in the rain: we could tie the horses to trees, and we would all just have to stay wet and hungry until the morning light. I did not relish the prospect, however, and was very relieved when we found a track which led us through a yard bordered by houses and finally back to the road. While Ali waited by the road with the mares for Richard, I returned to one of houses we had just passed, which had a light on, and banged on the door. I said 'Good evening' to the woman who answered, then immediately announced that I was English. Instant smiles and welcome – this is clearly the open sesame. I asked if we could put our horses and car in a barn I had seen, but was told it was locked. I must have looked downcast because one of the men in the office (it was the office of the local foresters) said they had three empty stables.

Richard went off with the woman, Lyuba, to get the key to the stable block, and in no time the horses were parked in tiny narrow stalls with masses of wonderful hay and their oats, warm and dry, and as happy as sandboys. The foresters had said we could sleep by the stove in their office, but that there would be people working there. In the end Lyuba insisted we stay with her next door, so Ali and I peeled the spuds while she milked the cow (I had a sense of *deja vu*) and we sat down to a wonderful meal of tomatoes with *smetana* (soured cream), fried eggs and pork fat, spuds and raw garlic.

Belarus houses appear more substantial than Russian houses, but it is an illusion. The side facing out may be brick, but the other sides are wooden, and inside is the same squalor and lack of facilities. For example, there was no running water here either, and Lyuba cooked in the porch.

Lyuba's husband, Edvard was hopelessly drunk even when we arrived. I just couldn't understand him through the very strong Belarus accent and the slurring, but as long as we smiled or laughed, he was content. It turned out he was a farrier but, although we had several loose shoes, I was not inclined to let him touch my horses.

While I tried to make polite conversation, Ali was writing her diary. Lyuba and Edvard were stunned – why was she using the

wrong hand? I was assured that in the whole of Russia and
Belarus there was not one single person who wrote using their
left hand, and indeed I had some difficulty convincing our kind
hosts that in the West there were a lot of people who were left-
handed, including my own daughter.

28 September – DAY 64
Lyuba pressed on us a delicious breakfast (macaroni served as
porridge, with milk and sugar, fried spuds and tomato salad, and
tea) and we rode off at 8am. Lyuba would take no money for anything, so we gave her a box of chocolate mints and said many
thanks.

It was still raining when we set out, but the weather improved
gradually, although it was very windy. We were stuck with riding on the main road, but Pompeii behaved well, on the whole,
except when another oncoming lorry pulled out to overtake. I led
Masha who had the handbrake on, as usual. Unfortunately, the
ride was extremely boring as there was forest all around, so we
had no view, and the land was as flat as the Fens. We are well
into autumn now, with leaves swirling off the trees like snow in
a blizzard.

The afternoon was also boring, but we covered about fifty-
three kilometres today, which was not bad going considering we
started two hours late and the evenings are really drawing in
now. The campsite Richard found is OK, but there is not enough
grazing, so we have upped the horses' oat ration.

29 September – DAY 65
Had to get up at 2am for a pee, but I didn't go far as I couldn't
find my head-torch, I was naked and there was a freezing wind!
The door to my bivvy-bag was facing the wind (which had
veered in the night) so it took quite a while for me to warm up
again.

Ghastly start to the day, straight into the really biting wind.
Richard gave us a hot drink about 9am, which was very welcome. Gradually the sun tried (but failed) to fight its way
through the clouds, although it did become slightly less cold. We
cross the main road (right to Leeda, straight on to Grodna) after
which we were astounded by the first bit of good manners we

have yet met on the part of a driver – a man was driving a cater-pillar tractor on the verge, so I pulled up to say to Ali that we ought to cross the road to avoid him, but he had stopped to let us pass!

Lorries and cars hurtle past, but Pompeii is now only seriously silly when oncoming lorries pull out to overtake. Some lorries do pull out a little to pass us, if they can. We are seeing more and more foreign-registered lorries (mainly Dutch, but yesterday we even came across two from Teheran in a transport café, and today we saw some removal vans from Cheltenham). We also see many expensive foreign makes of car, notably Mercedes and BMW.

The rubbish beside the road is now much more Westernized too – fewer rusty old farm implements and more empty packets of Marlboro and crisp packets.

Another aside: since I left Alexikovo (about 2090 kilometres ago), I have seen the following road casualties: two hedgehogs, four dogs, a cat and a bird – and one of the hedgehog corpses was on a track. On the other hand, we have seen at least fifty roadside memorials, usually to young people, which mark the spot of their deaths.

Pompeii, who had already lost his near-fore shoe, today lost his near-hind shoe also and went lame on the near fore, so I got off and walked. The mares have each lost a hind shoe.

We finally left that dreadful road at about 3.45pm and can look forward to a good stretch of side roads before we join another main road into Grodna. We have been on main roads since before Minsk.

Towards the end of the day, as we rode through a small vil-lage, we were hailed by a local. I took the opportunity to ask if there was a farrier nearby. One was found, but he refused to do it. We shrugged and started to ride away, but his friends per-suaded him to change his mind and Pompeii has a new shoe (and they did not use ropes to lash him up).

Now in bed, trying to work up the courage to take off my clothes: the wind has gone and it is freezing. I hope the horses will be all right, they sound very happy chomping.

30 September – DAY 66
Bitterly cold, frosty start, and we left just after 6.30am. Richard

went to try to phone Giles, and we made good progress, happy to be in the countryside. We passed several churches, including one huge red brick one, with spires instead of onion domes, that could have been a cathedral in Germany.

Richard finally caught us up at about 10.30am, and we stopped soon afterwards for a hot drink. All the people working in the fields of mangel-wurzels, who looked exactly like creatures in a Breughel painting, came to chat and told us there were some stables near Grodna for our day off. There was yet another example of the honesty of these people. I offered to buy some mangel-wurzels. 'No, no, we cannot sell them to you because they belong to the Collective Farm.' When I said that we only wanted a few to give to the horses, they promptly said, 'In that case you can have some' – it never occurred to any of them that they could have made a few bucks on the side.

Nasty driving rain and sleet followed that stop, and the wind had resumed full strength, but Richard found a sheltered spot for lunch.

Belarus has been a real watershed: not only it is a transition from East to West, but now when I tell my story, people are astonished by how far I have already been as they are by how far I am going. For some reason, I have been forgetting to worry about my expired Belarus visa. The policemen who had looked at my passport have said nothing, and so I shall keep quiet until I am caught.

Also, there are no stones in the parts of Russia I have been through, but during the last couple of weeks we have encountered them for the first time. About a week ago when I was leading Pompeii to his tether, he freaked out and tore himself out of my hand – he had seen some boulders!

1 October – DAY 67
Slept well, and woke when Richard got up. The howling gale sent our table flying, and that set the tone to the day's riding.

We mounted up and left at 6.30am in the hope of finding a cup of something hot at a café signposted as being ten kilometres down the road – but there was no café to be found. We were stopped, first by some nice policemen who wished us *'bon voyage'*, then by a very fierce policeman who studied all our documents with great care, and then smiled and also wished us *'bon voyage'*.

No sign of Richard until about 10am, when it turned out that he had found excellent stables only a mile from Grodna. We arrived shortly before 2pm, with me getting worried about Pompeii who, after being so full of oats that he has been jogging for the last couple of days, is taking incredibly short steps. Could it be the result of having his frog trimmed when he was shod the other day? He is not lame, and trots readily enough – I pray that a rest this afternoon and a night in a warm stable with plenty of hay will help.

The horses have a relatively easy time of it for about a week, as tomorrow we only have about thirty-two kilometres to go to where we plan to camp so that we can be at the border as early as possible. The nags can rest while I do battle, first with the Belarus authorities and then with the Polish ones. We hope to find a Polish farmer who can stable them for a night or two soon after we cross the border so that we can go to the hotel in Bialystok with Giles.

At the stables here at Grodna they breed miniature horses, and in the stables Ali and I fell in love with a three-week-old foal who was smaller than my Rhodesian Ridgeback dog. His mother was only about eight or nine hands high.

We are in the hotel in Grodna now, which is pretty luxurious by our new low standards. I complained that there was no hot water, to be told after some enquiries (during which we had lunch) that I had not let it run long enough. Lunch was fine – they had whisky and cognac, but no chicken. When Ali asked for milk in her coffee she was told 'Nyet' – incomprehensible in a country where we have seen dozens of dairy herds in the last fortnight, and cows grazing within a few hundred yards of the city centre.

Early supper degenerated into a wine-drinking session and we danced the night away in the hotel disco!

2 October – DAY 68
Woke with a hangover. Felt worse after breakfast, but felt a hundred percent as soon as I got into the saddle. The horses must have been well fed because Pompeii was looking out over his stable door and ignoring his hay. They had self-filling water bowls, but we realized when they drank thirstily from the first puddle we saw that the horses had not understood how they worked.

We were stopped by the police just outside Grodna. They thought we were gypsies, and were vastly intrigued by our journey.

We set off into the countryside, and as we were trotting along the road, a convoy of four German cars and vans passed, and took photographs of us, clearly assuming we were natives. They stopped a bit further on and I could not help it, I told them when we caught them up that we were not Russian or Belarussian, but English, and I had quite a long conversation with the leader. My German ran out very quickly and I ended up telling him about the trip in Russian. They were part of a humanitarian aid group.

At about 5pm in a village, we asked about stables. 'Yes', I was told, 'There is plenty of room in some stables where they keep horses.' When I found the woman concerned, the answer was '*Nyet*' because the horses and the stables there belonged to the state and she didn't have the authority to let us stay. Richard found a lovely spot, sheltered (it had become very cold after a lovely sunny start) and with good grazing. There is only one snag – we can be seen from the road. Only eight kilometres to the border. Must put on some make-up before doing battle with the authorities – I must say I am dreading that part. Then Giles will be waiting on the other side.

CHAPTER TEN

Poland with Ali

3 October – DAY 69

I am writing this a day late as I had no time yesterday – we are now in Poland. We got up as usual, and I applied some make-up by torchlight, and we were off by 6.45am. Richard hurried to join us, and we got to the border about 8.10am, causing a great deal of interest as we trotted resolutely past all the cars in the queue. As I had feared, they changed shifts at 8am but they were changing as we arrived, so we had to wait for half an hour. We then sat for another half an hour while they calmly set about some heavy roadworks. During this time many of the officials spoke to us, and I tried to be as polite as possible to them all.

Eventually, a very senior, rather Prussian-looking, officer arrived and spoke to us in English. What made us think we were allowed to take these horses out of Belarus, he wanted to know. 'We have permission', I replied. 'What permission?' he barked. 'Well, we have permission to cross Poland and I have already paid the duty on the horses.' 'Show me the documents!' Richard duly produced the file and the important man grunted and then, to my great relief, I heard him telling his minions that all was in order and that I had paid my dues.

We were allowed through to the next stage, and a young official asked us to follow him. I was then grilled by a fat, pasty Customs official while the border vet had a look at the veterinary certificate. She was as nice as he was unpleasant, and when we had to wait, she insisted Ali and I went for coffee in the warmth of her office.

While the Customs man played backgammon, we waited . . . In the meantime, the horses ate and ate (there was plenty of good grazing) and had a lovely rest. After about four hours we finally got everything right and rode across No Man's Land to the Polish border. Huge smiles all round and we were told to wait for the official vet – and there was Giles waving like a lunatic. They let him through, hugs, kisses and tears all round, and the horses were left to graze again while Andy, Giles's taxi driver, went to fetch the duty vet.

The sun had emerged after a misty start, and we waited comfortably until Andy and very *sympathique* vet arrived. Giles was over the moon, said I looked healthy and glowing. For some extraordinary reason, he had expected me to look thin, pale and wan – after living outdoors for two months? More documents were required, produced and signed by the vet, and we then rode to some stables at the local veterinary surgery, where some blood samples were taken for Giles to take back to the Central Veterinary Laboratories in England, and the horses were settled in really lovely stables.

Off to the hotel, all OK (except my right little toe hurts). Bed(!) and a shower, and then Richard and Ali arrived for the share-out of goodies, but Giles had not been able to find the warm pullovers, and Ali's knickers and Puffa that she had asked for.

4 October – DAY 70

Awoke at 4pm in pain from my back so I woke Giles – more brilliant sex. After breakfast Giles went off to the station with Andy, but the train had been cancelled. In the end Richard drove Giles to Warsaw while Andy took us to pick up the farrier who had promised to shoe all the horses. Andy had to hold their legs up while Ali and I held their heads. Even here there are no horse shoes, so we had to use the English ones.

A totally mad man called Heinrich insisted we buy one of his heavy horses – I told him I did not have enough money, but he said we could pay later. I told him that far too many documents would be needed to get it into the EC. A woman called Sophie, who turned out to be a friend of Marek's and who speaks a little French, invited us for tea. We went, leaving Andy to wait for Richard to return from Warsaw and bring him to Sophie's farm.

Sophie was ashamed at the lack of luxury in her charming home, thinking we would compare it with our own houses in the West. Ali and I were at pains to point out that her home was a palace compared with what we were used to, and I think and hope Sophie's embarrassment was mollified. While we were helping her to prepare the tea, Heinrich turned up with a bottle of pink champagne. Like many Poles, he wears a tattered trilby which makes them all look like spivs on a racecourse. He had noticed Ali was not wearing a wedding ring, and as he combed his hair he told me he was a 'cavalier' – looking for a wife?

Worried about Richard, we returned to the surgery to find him on the phone from Bialystok by which time the vets had insisted we sleep in the surgery. Everyone has been incredibly kind and hospitable, but I have had to speak French, German and Russian by turns, getting hopelessly mixed up, and the Poles have quite a thick accent when speaking Russian. The Polish language is a nightmare – I have had to write down phrases in Cyrillic script – and listening to the locals is very confusing as I keep hearing incomprehensible babble interspersed with well-known Russian words.

5 October – DAY 71
We left at 6.15am, with the horses in fine fettle, so we did thirty miles very easily. The Poles we pass in towns and villages are all very interested in us, but so far I have only learned a few phrases, although Polish is similar enough to Russian for me to understand the basic questions we get asked.

We saw lots of horses being transported in open trailers and decided there was a sale somewhere. In Solowicja we had to stop because Richard wanted to check a road that allegedly went through the marshes to Kuligi (cutting about thirty kilometres [eighteen miles] off the journey) and Ali wanted to ring Marek. No answer from Marek, and Richard spent an hour failing to find a way through. The whole time I was standing there with the three horses I had a river of Poles flowing up, asking questions, reeling back stunned when I managed to explain what we were doing. There were many drunken men (there had been a horse market there today), and some interested schoolgirls, one of whom spoke a little English and French.

From the moment we crossed the border, this was obviously a very different country, even the topography is different. There are nice, tidy houses with nice, tidy gardens, and fences everywhere (yuck), and although Polish drivers hurtle past as though we are not there, just as in Russia (unfortunately Pompeii has started freaking out again), the shops have goods in them.

There have been no frosts here yet, as I see the dahlias are still alive and flowering. The weather since we crossed the border has been warm and sunny, and it seems we have turned the clock back at least a fortnight, which is wonderful. I am sitting here typing this an hour after sunset, but I am only wearing a pullover – amazing.

I do wish Ali wouldn't always urge her horse on ahead. I know Pompeii lags behind, but he still has short strides and anyway I don't want to spend the whole journey pushing him on hard. That said, she is an interesting and extremely amusing companion.

Must get up at 3am to use all available daylight, so to bed now.

6 October – DAY 72

We did get up at 3am, but it turned out to be too early and we then had to wait around for daylight.

We started along the main road, while the cars still have their lights on. We arrived at Szlabin as the sun came up, and we gave the horses a drink from a tin bath in a cow meadow, with a farmer in a tractor looking on. I did ask him for permission, but got no answer.

Through Szlabin, then immediately Richard steered us on to minor roads and sandy tracks through beautiful forests and countryside. We arrived at Kuligi at about noon, to a warm welcome from Hannya, Marek's wife. Their house is amazing – huge, all wood, and based on a traditional Polish design – but it is not finished yet as they are doing almost all the work themselves and Marek has had problems with his spine. The house boasts a hanging bed and cot, a wooden bath, wooden blinds, and it's wonderful. We are staying in an ancient cottage in the garden because their seventeen-month-old son (also called Marek) cries all night and keeps visitors awake. The cottage is quite delightful, but has no running water.

Horses were initially staked out by the house, but when Marek returned, we put them further away on lovely clover-rich grazing, where we hope they will feed well and get yet more rest. I checked at 9.30pm, and all seemed peaceful in the light of a nearly full moon.

Marek breeds Polish marsh-ponies, and by an amazing coincidence is just about to send some to Suffolk on loan to the Suffolk Wildlife Trust!

Our clothes have all been washed in a washing machine, and are now drying by the warmth of a stove which Marek lit for us in the cottage.

7 October – DAY 73

Ali and I watered and fed horses, and I sat around in my dressing gown for a while, being idle. We ate a delicious breakfast, then I scrubbed the numnahs and girth sleeves, and Richard kindly helped me. Ali went to Warsaw with Marek, then later on Richard and I went to change money, look at shops, and have a drink in Elk. Sadly we must be off again tomorrow.

8 October – DAY 74

Marek and his friend, Tadeusz asked why I had chosen Frankfurt am Oder as the crossing point. I told them that to get to Holland, as originally planned, it was in a straight line, but I immediately saw that now we were sailing from Hamburg, it made no sense.

Rang Giles to get him to ask Bernard van Goethem in Brussels if it would be a problem to enter the EC at Szczecin, and Marek has promised to contact the Polish Veterinary Services as my vet permission to cross Poland specifies Bialystok and Slubice as the entry and exit points.

Marek and Hannya have been so kind, and there were heartfelt thanks when we left, but we may see him again tomorrow night as we hope to park the horses with a friend of theirs.

We finally got going and thankfully the weather is still good. The horses were fresh and full of energy, and we did about forty kilometres before we ran out of daylight at about 4pm. The countryside is stunningly beautiful, and Richard found some lovely tracks, but I am so disappointed by the number of fences and ditches which prevent us from leaving the road or taking the shortest line across country. This may be Eastern Europe but it has far more in common with England in that respect than it has with Russia. I am also frustrated by not really being able to chat with locals, although I did managed to convey what we were doing to a couple of men who were out shooting.

9 October – DAY 75

Up soon after 3.30am, dressed, had breakfast, etc. We were in the saddle by 5.15am. We only had two one-hour stops, and we moved quite fast, and I feel sure we did at least sixty-five kilometres (forty miles). Our journey brought us a bit of everything, country roads, forest tracks (where we spotted some cranes flying overhead), main roads and towns. The weather has been glorious. Marek, Hannya and the baby caught us up at our last stop, and told us it was only thirty-two kilometres (twenty miles) to their friends' house, but it took us three and a half hours with a lot of trotting, so Ali and I both feel sure it was further. It was getting dangerously dark by the time we arrived. Ali railed at some rudeness of Richard's. She was very close to tears, but I said I could do nothing. Apparently she had asked him what she was doing wrong, to which he had no answer (of course). Those two personalities just clash and there's an end to it; nobody can do anything about it.

Marek's friends were very welcoming, and gave us a really lovely barbecue supper by a huge bonfire under the full moon. These people are vets, but the change from communism has made life very hard for them, and it is difficult to get by – in fact, Marek had provided the meat we were eating. They are trying to make a little extra money by breeding dogs.

There was no time to put up our awning, so we all hope it doesn't rain in the night. Exhausted now (9.30pm) and in bivvy.

10 October – DAY 76

Richard gave us breakfast, and there was complete silence from the house until the children went off to school. Then Annya gave us coffee and we saw ten dachshund puppies, none of which she had been able to sell. The prettiest dog, though, was a very pretty and sweet young (three-month-old) Bavarian Bloodhound, who looked (apart from no ridge) remarkably like a Rhodesian Ridgeback puppy.

When we left circumstances forced us to use the road (where I refuse to trot except in an emergency) so we didn't make much distance. After that, Richard found forest tracks and for the rest of the day we rode through stunningly beautiful countryside, with tracks winding up and down hill – a vast improvement on Russia's straight tracks along mainly flat ground.

In this way we made up some ground. The weather was by now seriously hot – we simply can't believe it after the Belarus cold, wind, rain and frost. The dahlias in people's gardens are still flourishing, so there can't have been any frosts yet.

This area is full of lakes, which does not help Richard's navigation but is very easy on the eye. Nothing dramatic, just gentle beauty. We are all fantasizing about buying a farm and land and operating riding, sailing and/or adventure holidays. It is now very late and we are sitting round a lovely camp fire, wearing only T-shirts. The moon, now very slightly on the wane, which rose dark orange, has now resumed normal moon hue and is flooding the countryside. I could stay forever.

11 October – DAY 77
Up at 3.30am, left in thick mist at 5.25am. Met a man in the forest, but we are now sufficiently *au fait* with local customs to assume he was a mushroom-gatherer and not a rapist, a correct assumption as it turned out.

The mist only lifted at breakfast and then we had another gloriously hot, sunny day. Beautiful riding through forests and round lakes, but it was frustrating at times, as we lost Richard once for an hour in the middle of the day, (he went round a marshy bit that we could get through but he couldn't), and we wasted some time trying to get round a lake.

In the morning, while riding along a road in a village, a car passed us and screeched to a halt. 'Police!' I thought, but no, the back door opened and out stepped a six-year-old – it was the school run. I keep forgetting we are no longer in Russia.

12 October – DAY 78
Yet again we are enjoying the views over glorious countryside, all the more so for the brilliant autumn foliage.

Ali and I both stopped for a pee early on, and tried to take a shortcut back to the road. To our surprise we found ourselves in a barracks full of soldiers, so we calmly made our way down the drive to the astonishment of the two guards on the gate. They did not challenge us, but we tried to imagine the conversation in the mess.

There are some strange contrasts in this country. There are

some poor villages but also, something never seen in Russia, decent-sized houses, probably farmhouses, on their own in the country, houses one would actually be prepared to live in. I also saw yesterday a ghastly executive housing estate. Also new in Poland are satellite dishes.

The tracks and ungraded roads we are using, like in Russia, have hoof prints only in the middle, meaning that they are used only by horses being driven, rather than ridden. The carts here often only have one shaft, on the right of the horse, which I should have thought would make the poor beasts dreadfully lop-sided. We have not seen a ridden horse for weeks – certainly not in Poland – and I have still not seen a woman rider since I left Alexikovo.

Overall an enjoyable day in which we hardly put a foot on tar-mac and spent the whole time riding through incredibly beauti-ful forests. From the progress point of view, we did not do well – by lunch time we had covered nearly thirty-two kilometres on the ground but only just over seventeen kilometres as the crow flies. After lunch it was worse, when I misunderstood Richard and we went for about four or five kilometres in the wrong direc-tion before he caught us up. We are now in a lovely site (except it is bang next to the road, which is really just a tiny country lane), on the edge of the forest but looking out over open hills, with the horses on the hillside below us. I do hope Masha is sensible tonight as at lunch-time today, she rolled and got in a hopeless tangle with the rope not only wrapped twice round her off-hind but actually inserted between shoe and hoof!

With the renewal of summer weather, of course, we are suffer-ing dreadfully from mosquitoes and the re-emergence of the dreaded tick.

13 October – DAY 79

The weather has changed for the worse – windy and cold, and the sun never appeared. We rode for some time (three hours or so) in the forest, then on to roads for the rest of the day. Richard left arrows to show us the way, but we missed the best clue – a message in a jam jar hanging from a tree. We noticed the jam jar but didn't stop to see the message.

Road work was boring and dangerous with Pompeii, and slow because we can't trot. Delicious burger lunch cooked by Richard

– which we ate late because he had been to phone Giles. Unfortunately the only news he had was that the Germans won't let us through anywhere except Frankfurt-am-Oder. Very unusually we all had a drink, and decided to go via Sweden instead of through Germany. Richard had bought Ali and me a present each – a really lovely amber and silver crucifix.

After another hour or so, Richard found some people at a farm to give the horses water, and luckily they spoke Russian, and were quite amazed at the length of our trip. I tried to sober up, surely we should stick to the original plan and go through Germany?

During supper, Richard and Ali convinced me that the route of Gdansk-Ystad ferry, then ride to Gothenburg, then ferry to Harwich makes the best sense. It was decided that tomorrow Ali should ring her friend, the Countess, in Sweden for advice, and also call Marek to find out about the Polish rules, etc. What will Giles say? He is a great Swedophile and speaks the language, so I hope he'll approve.

14 October – DAY 80

The plan was to ride to the post office and make our calls from there, but as we passed the farm, the wife told us the post office would be closed (Saturday). Never mind, she said, I will ring them and tell them to open up for you. When we got there it was unequivocally closed, and she came bustling up on her bike to explain that there had been nobody there when she rang.

In the end we put the horses in their paddock, and the farmer gave them a huge pile of lovely hay, and we tried making our calls from their kitchen, but there was no answer from anyone.

The farmer's wife told us about her daughter (who was there), who had been ill for three years with cancer and who was now getting better thanks to a *tisane* made from a fungus which grows on birch trees. This ancient Polish remedy is so successful it is being sold to the Germans. She also told us she needed a new right hip (having already had the left one replaced) but that it would cost twenty million old Zloties (£555). It seems their health care and education have disintegrated since the collapse of communism. They are having a general election soon, and have seventeen parties to choose from. Lech Walesa does not seem too popular.

I was enjoying myself hugely and I think it must have showed, the wife said I looked happy but that Ali looked exhausted. For the first time she was not taken for my daughter, which made a refreshing change: as she is only fifteen years younger than I am, my morale has suffered several blows in the past.

These kind people did tell us about some excellent stables thirty kilometres (eighteen miles) away, so we set off at noon and had some glorious cross-country riding, albeit in the drizzle. We had nearly rejoined the main road when Richard was halted because the track we had been following ended in a farmyard and he could go no further. We couldn't face the long trek round so I boldly asked a man if we could ride as far as the road, to which he agreed, clearly thinking the question was unnecessary. We found a barbed wire fence which Ali dismantled and then reinstated after we had passed through.

Unfortunately the last stretch was a nightmare rush along the busy main road as the sun set and it got scarily darker by the minute. The Polish roads are really hazardous: what I took to be the hard shoulder is actually another lane which slow vehicles use while being overtaken. Having got to the stud, and negoti- ated with an extremely arrogant director, we then had to travel down a country lane. We were following a chap called Voytek in his car and protected from the rear by Richard in the Toyota. It is the first time I have been chatted up by a man in a car while walk- ing beside my horse.

Once the horses were settled, Voytek took Ali and me to a very posh and expensive hotel in Ostroda where we checked in. After a disgusting supper, we went to the night-club. Beer-keller music did nothing for us, but the Poles danced happily enough in a sort of clockwork way. To my amazement, a Communards number was played (I danced with Richard), after which the quality of the music did improve. A cheerful chap we christened 'Mr Belly' (for obvious reasons) danced indefatigably with every woman in the room (having politely asked Richard's permission to dance first with Ali and later with me). I was able to explain about my expedition, and he laughed and told me I was an *amazonka* – nobody has ever accused me of being an Amazon before. [I was to find out later that *amazonka* actually means horsewoman.]

15 October – DAY 81

Giles rang. He had somehow procured the telephone number for Polish Prestige, a company which ships horses from Poland to Sweden. He seemed in good form, and asked me about getting Rada to England, so after breakfast I faxed him the document I signed in Lisky and suggested he contact Sasha to see if anything be done, but I said that although she was a good horse, she was not worth spending a lot more money on.

16 October – DAY 82

The phone went soon after breakfast, and it was Marcin at Polish Prestige and he was very helpful, faxing me the phone numbers of some stables in Sopot (near Gdansk) and of the veterinary laboratory in Sweden.

I rang the laboratory who thought the British tests would be accepted by the Swedes, and gave me the number of the Swedish Department of Agriculture. Needless to say, the woman in charge of the relevant section had the day off, so I sent a fax explaining all and saying that Richard or I would ring on or after Tuesday. I also faxed the stables at Sopot and requested directions, and asked if they could find a lorry to transport the horses to Sweden. They immediately faxed back a detailed map.

During supper Katie rang and we have arranged for her to fly to Gdansk on Saturday evening and she will ride the rest of the way home, because Ali has already spent about three weeks longer away from home than she had intended.

17 October – DAY 83

I had a shower – the last for some time, I suspect. Had breakfast and paid the bill – nearly £500! Most of that was phone calls, but I am now getting worried about money as I fear the ferries will be expensive. No more hotels for us.

We left the stables at 8.30am and had an excellent morning's ride. There were some road works but also lots of really beautiful tracks. Pompeii in particular was full of bounce after his rest – indeed I twice let him and Muffin canter, and had the greatest difficulty in applying the brakes to either horse. His near-hind shoe, which has never really fitted, is now clanking loose.

After a brief lunch we set off again: we have decided to have only one break during the day now that the extended nights give the horses a longer rest. The weather was perfect for riding – dry, coolish, but with some hazy sunshine.

Towards the end of the day we found ourselves in what could have been East Anglia – huge fields and apparently modern farming methods – yuck. The landscape was saved visually by being very rounded, with lots of small hillocks.

We came round a corner to find Richard asking some locals about a track towards the next village. This village looks very poor. We had remarked to each other as we rode in that a lot of the farmyards looked almost Russian in their squalid appearance, but unlike in Russia, there were loads of children. No doubt here that this is a Catholic country.

The man Richard was speaking to turned out to be the farm foreman, called Tkacz, and he spoke Russian. I asked about stables, and am writing this in the farmyard (because I am smoking), with the horses tied up in some stalls in a wonderful old brick building. We were told to help ourselves to straw for the horses and ourselves (we too are to sleep in some stalls), and these kind people have produced the equivalent of about two bales of hay each for the horses – and won't hear of accepting any payment. The boss, Antoni Galecki, appeared, and was as kind and welcoming as Tkacz, and we have exchanged addresses. We have eaten and plan to put our sleeping bags on straw mattresses. We were also given fresh milk (there are about twenty cows here), also without payment.

The straw came from another beautiful old building. Antoni told me that it used to house sheep, but that there are now almost no sheep in Poland. 'We had noticed how few there were', I said, 'but why?' 'We get very cheap wool.' 'From where?' 'Australia.' 'But what about meat?' 'Polish people don't like lamb. Best of all we like pork, then beef. Lamb is the last choice.'

Antoni has a daughter, Paulina, who is studying English but was too shy to say anything beyond 'Hello'. I shall not be surprised to get a phone call from Poland in a few years' time. In spite of the apparent poverty of this area, about seventy kilometres (forty-three miles) south-east of Gdansk, there are very many neglected large old brick houses and barns, any one of which could be made very beautiful. The houses tend to be rather Georgian in appearance, very well-proportioned and symmetrical, with the front door plumb centre.

18 October – DAY 84

A dreadful night. Every time a horse lay down or got up it made such a noise we all woke up thinking the worst. Pompeii got free at some stage and started making a pass at Muffin, and I rushed over when I heard a crash which sounded as though all the horses had fallen over at once, but there was nothing wrong.

We left just before 6am, these kind people having helped us to water the horses. It took us a while to pick up the right track. After that we covered thirty kilometres before we got to Marienbad, which had a beautiful castle and church in a walled keep. We travelled a bit further before we found some grazing and waited there for Richard, who had gone to phone the Swedish Board of Agriculture – but he had waited forty-five minutes before giving up. We must have done forty-eight kilometres (thirty miles) today but we are still forty kilometres from Gdansk. Is this *Through the Looking Glass* country?

Within an hour of setting out this morning, we could have been in Lincolnshire – the countryside is as flat as a pancake.

A totally drunk Pole found us at our campsite this evening and refused to leave for ages. He was not deterred by our lack of understanding, but stayed for about an hour and a half talking happily. He wanted to buy Masha (who he thought was a stallion) and then to take Ali and me home to sleep and meet his wife. He was very insistent and grabbed us both by the arms, Richard nearly had to intervene. He only left after we had eaten and I pretended to fall asleep.

19 October – DAY 85

Left at 6am. Pompeii didn't want to get up (I suspect the foul water that was all we could find last night) and has lost both his hind shoes.

Yet another truly awful day. We were forced to go along roads most of the time, although we were able to ride along a dyke for a while until we were defeated by electric fencing. Even when we went into a field to trot, we had to retrace our steps as it was surrounded by a ditch.

After we had crossed a very wide river on an extremely long bridge, we got on to the dyke on the other side. No sooner had we done so than we were hailed by a Pole who desperately wanted to buy Masha. I told him we were in a hurry, but he showed me his house and asked us to go there later. When we arrived at the other end of the dyke he was there waiting for us, having driven round by road. He said he wanted Masha for his daughter, aged three or four. I took his name, but don't think he would pay the US $3020 (£2000-odd) I want for her.

Things degenerated and we had to ride along ever busier roads, culminating in what must have been the most dangerous road so far. It was very narrow, with absolutely no verge, but a great deal of traffic hurtling past, and Pompeii naturally decided to shy (into the road) at trees.

By lunch-time I was in a lot of pain – driving Pompeii on, trying to keep him on the edge of the road, dragging Masha – my back was tortured and twisted.

On separate occasions today we met two drunks in their sixties who thought we were marvellous and tried to help. The second one said he had been a farrier for forty years but shoes were no longer available. He picked up Pompeii's feet and said we needed more shoes before we went much further, which is quite true. Thank goodness he didn't notice the hind shoes were missing.

We didn't make it to the stables. Richard found a lovely sheltered camp site in the woods, and Ali and I went to the stables to explain that we had been delayed. The roads were awful, very busy, and the Sopot Hipodrom was hard to find. People here speak English (Gdansk and Gdynia are ports), so we asked at a kiosk for the Hipodrom. A young man told me the way, then suddenly appeared in his car and guided us there. The man on the gate had heard of us, and directed us to a stable block about a quarter of a mile away, but the only person I could find was a German-speaking young man. I asked him to pass on the message that we would arrive with the horses tomorrow.

On way back it started raining. Richard, having been very cheerful since the day we arrived in Poland, has been in a foul mood for two days – why?

20 October – DAY 86
Up at 4.30am, and waited for the light. We made very poor progress as we had to wait for Richard to scout ahead all the time. In what was marked on the map as a village, which was actually a busy town, Richard appeared and told us the way – ten

kilometres (six miles) of six-lane highway. In the end we did a kilometre or so, which was not so bad because there was a good verge, then we dived off sideways. We then had to do another kilometre or two along another busy road, by which time I had half-jokingly suggested we ride up the beach. Damn me if Richard didn't take us there. The weather was still very windy, and at about the time we got to the beach it started raining. Ali and I had loads of childish fun on the beach, with the horses spooking at the waves, and then we galloped off and left Richard still videoing. Following hoof prints in the sand and asking locals, we found the stables. The boss, Krzysztof, was very kind and welcoming, and the horses were put into wonderful loose boxes. Then we began to feel concerned that there was still no sign of Richard.

More in hope than expectation of success, Ali tried him on the walkie-talkie (which we had not been able to use before because he had told us the batteries were both flat) and made contact, to our great surprise and delight. He turned up later, glum.

While waiting for Richard to turn up, our new friend asked about hotels for us, and we said we had not booked anything yet. He offered us a flat there, at the Hipodrom, but apologized that it was not of a very high standard. We said we were accustomed to the forest or to Russian hotels. He took us to a very nice two-roomed flat with sofa beds, a shower and loo, and walked off saying, 'You are my guests, there is no charge for this'. Wow.

Reunited with Richard and squeaky clean after tepid showers, we went to Krzysztof's office to try to phone the Swedish Board of Agriculture people. No luck. In the meantime we asked about a farrier (they actually have German horse shoes here), a vet (they have their own one in residence) and a lorry to transport the horses in the ferry (the helpful German-speaking man I spoke to last night has a lorry). To our horror we also found out that the Gdansk-Ystad ferry no longer runs (or runs only in summer). We may be able to drive them from Oxelösund by lorry to Stockholm but we will not know until Monday which is three days away.

Ali wanted a swim and I wanted a massage, having discovered that both were available at the hotel. I was not sure how much to undress, so I just left my knickers on, and was a bit surprised to find the masseur was a man. He did a brilliant job, however. I think he was a proper sports masseur, and I felt wonderfully relaxed.

Ali and I had a couple of drinks and went back to our flat, by which time it was about 9.15pm and, to my horror, the stable gates were shut. Fortunately the gate-keeper was still on duty and opened them for us. Richard was not amused, wanting to know if we had eaten, but we were still full from lunch.

So after we had seen to the horses (who still don't know how to operate automatic drinking systems), he went off to find a hamburger, not returning for about three hours.

CHAPTER ELEVEN

Poland with Katie

21 October – DAY 87

We all went to the hotel for breakfast where we met a very nice Polish girl called Kate, who joined us at our table.

Up and off to the ferry port, where they confirmed that we can only sail to Oxelösund or Karlskrona in Sweden from Gdansk or Gdynia, so we have to sort something out with the Swedish authorities. If they are adamant then the only thing we can do is ride to Szczecin and cross into Germany.

Ali and I then played tourist and wandered around mediaeval Gdansk, which was amazing. Every house looked incredibly old, but we were told that the whole town had been rebuilt after the war. It was not the Germans who had done the damage, they said, but the Russians. Every single shop sold amber, and there must have been tons of the stuff.

We had agreed with Kate that if she could find a room for the night she would meet us at the hotel at 6pm so we could have a drink and a meal before meeting my Katie at the airport – I can't believe how much I am looking forward to seeing her.

23 October – DAY 88

Well, all went as planned. We had a good dinner at the hotel then Ali, Kate and I took a taxi to the airport (where we saw one of the presidential candidates while we waited). Katie came through, and we all went back to the flat and talked for a while before Richard went out and dropped Kate off on the way.

Ali hesitated about going to the Countess at Klarsthorp, and for some reason seemed very upset ('I get the feeling I am in the way'). What on earth put that idea into her head? We begged her to stay, but in vain. Actually, I am really looking forward to spending some time alone with Katie, although of course I shall miss Ali.

Met Kate at the hotel and had lunch before I had to dash back to speak to Krzysztof's daughter, Adela about being interviewed for Polish television. As luck would have it, the camera crew turned up while Richard was taking Ali to the ferry (I felt awful about that, but I had agreed to the interview and couldn't let them down). Katie said I didn't make a fool of myself. Richard gave Adela a copy of the ITN video.

Tried a local seafood restaurant for dinner as a change from the hotel, where we discovered that the food was truly magnificent but the price was horrendous – about US $106 (£70) and we didn't get to bed until midnight. Richard is transformed and very relaxed – is it a mood swing or is it because Ali has gone? Time will tell.

Today was a very frustrating day. I spent over an hour trying to get through to Sweden. I tried again an hour later and got through on about the twentieth attempt, only to be met with a blank refusal to let the horses in at Oxelösund or at Karlskrona. I even offered to pay for a vet to go to either of those ports, but was informed that it was 'against our rules'. So we have to continue across Poland after all.

Saw Krzysztof and he got the stable vet along. He has taken two lots of blood samples: one lot Richard is getting a courier to take to the Ministry of Agriculture, Farming and Fisheries (MAFF) laboratories in Addlestone, and the other lot will be sent to a laboratory in Poland for analysis.

The farrier turned up, as promised, at about 2pm and I had to leave Katie to help him while I went to phone Giles at his office to ask if he could possibly ring van Goethem and find out if we can cross the border near Szczecin (Kolbaskowo) or ferry the horses into Kiel from Swinoujscie, and to ask him if it would be possible to keep our options open.

Back to the stables to find the farrier still shoeing Muffin, who was better behaved than usual, but not good. I have already notched up a US $75 (£50) bill for phones, 140 zloties (£39) for the vet, God knows how much for the farrier and the cost of stabling. The sooner we get back on the road, the cheaper (and healthier).

Later

Spoke to Giles, who has faxed a letter to Bengt Nordblom, an important chap in the Swedish Board of Agriculture, whose name the ever-helpful van Goethem had given him. I said that even if the Swedes did relent, it was too late – by making us hang around for two different vets, the blood samples will have expired by the time we get into the EC.

So, the plan is to ride to Swinoujscie and ferry the horses to Kiel, box them to Hamburg and ferry them to Harwich. I feel it is a cop-out not to ride at all in Germany, but everyone says it is just a case of being too dangerous for the horses.

24 October – DAY 89

It was slightly chaotic today. Richard mucked out and I said I would walk the horses round in turn as he did so, to help lessen the swelling on their legs caused by standing indoors. Pompeii first, on a headcollar, reared up quite soon and was nearly uncontrollable. I returned hastily and put his bridle on, but still had very little control, so I just walked him up and down outside our stable block. The mares weren't much better – Masha tried cantering on the spot and Muffin reared, and tried to tear away from me! It is time we moved on.

Richard and I went to ask Krzysztof for the bill and were astounded to be told that the horses, like us, were guests. The only thing we have to pay for is the cost of our phone calls. I also asked if we could buy oats, and was further told that they did not have such a financial crisis that they could not afford to let us have them as a gift. What generosity. We invited him to dinner tonight at the hotel.

As I emerged from the feed shed, a car screeched to a halt and I heard the driver say something about 'the English woman'. 'There she is,' pointed Krzysztof. Two serious and rather sinister men got out of the car and I thought 'Police. What have I done?', but it turned out they were journalists and wanted to interview and photograph me with Richard, Katie and the horses for a daily paper. Krzysztof will bring a copy early tomorrow morning, as we plan to leave around 7am.

Off to the hotel, where Richard and I had a swim and then a final, hot shower, while Katie just had the shower. Richard went back for Krzysztof and we had a slightly stiff dinner – we discovered that away from his beloved horses, he is actually not that easy to talk to.

25 October – DAY 90
Up at 4.30am to feed the horses and give them hay and water. First frost in Poland! Made a cup of tea, packed and tried to clean the flat. Katie and I mucked out while Richard packed the truck, and we had a final cup of coffee with Krzysztof in his office and paid for our phone calls (about US $90 [£60]).

Off about 8.15am, on a lovely ride through the forest. Katie rode Muffin, with me as usual on Pompeii. The tracks ended rather abruptly and we had to cross a very major road. Richard had the brilliant idea of setting us on a track next to the railway line, which went under the motorway. Almost as soon as we had emerged on the other side, though, the railway went over a tiny bridge crossing a dirt track. We would have had to walk between the rails, which I didn't fancy, so I dismounted and led Pompeii fifteen feet down an extremely steep (literally almost vertical) bank. I asked a bewildered old couple I met at the bottom to hold him while I rushed back up to grab Masha so that Katie could dismount and lead Muffin down. Talk about throwing Katie in at the deep end – she was absolutely horrified when Pompeii and I disappeared over the edge!

Apart from that episode we had a bit of everything – forest tracks where we got slightly lost, small towns, main roads and railways. We followed a track alongside the railway again for a while, and, after crossing a very dodgy metal bridge which even Pompeii didn't like and jogged across, we found ourselves on the station platform. It is lovely riding with Katie, she does not rush on ahead, and we have a lot to talk about after four months apart.

Tonight Katie was exhausted, while I was merely tired. After some problems, we found a campsite which is quite sheltered which is important because the weather today has been beautiful but windy. An old boy came up to interrogate us (as usual) and was very amiable.

As we are on the front page of the local paper, Richard just shows our copy to anyone who looks as though they may become stroppy.

26 October – DAY 91

Off at first light, but we turned the wrong way. Went well otherwise, Pompeii still being lively. We rode through some truly
lovely countryside and, after initial mist, we enjoyed a sunny
day. We had two short breaks (the second at Rati) and covered
about forty-eight kilometres (thirty miles). Richard went to
change money and shop while we searched for a campsite. It
appears there was no grazing for miles, so we are now sitting in
a small clearing in a forest with the horses chomping on our
penultimate bag of HorseHage.

Richard is flirting heavily with Katie, but she seems able
to cope.

27 October – DAY 92

Left at 6.45am, Katie on Masha again, I on Muffin to give Pompeii
a day off. We had to wait for Richard when we got to Stezyca to
be sure we didn't go wrong. Good day spent mainly along tracks
through forest. The sun tried to struggle through in the morning,
but only succeeded for a short while and at our second break it
started spitting with rain.

Richard found a good campsite, but we think the field the
horses are on, may actually be a plantation. We have increased
the oat ration, as we have decided in future to go back to having
only one break a day instead of two short ones: this will save a lot
of time spent hammering in tethers, untacking, then tacking up
and retrieving tether stakes. Katie reckons her bum can cope. She
is doing amazingly well, considering she had no time to try and
get fit, although she has cheated to the extent of using a sheep-
skin saddle-saver.

Tonight I cooked and Katie put up my tent as she is cold and
claustrophobic in the bivvy bag. She was very polite and apolo-
getic about being cold, so of course Richard is truly sympathetic.

28 October – DAY 93

We got into the saddles at 6.30am, and had a good day on the
whole, with lots of trotting with which the horses, with extra
oat rations, seemed happy and which Katie says is better for
her back. Today we were following some very wriggly tracks,
so although we covered a lot of ground, we only achieved

about thirty-seven kilometres (twenty-three miles) as the crow flies.

I am now sitting in a really lovely campsite in a village. Richard has found this beautiful grazing behind a derelict house, so I asked a village woman who, in spite of my telling her I was English and didn't understand Polish, answered with a flood of her native language out of which I picked the word 'Yes'. A little while later a man appeared with a huge armful of seasoned logs because they all thought we would be too cold. I may say they made the best camp fire ever.

Katie is warm at last in her tent, but the sheer volume of her overnight stuff is as embarrassing as Ali's – she has her rucksack, tent, karrimat, airbag, blanket and smelly pink eiderdown.

29 October – DAY 94

We endured a very cold night, and I took a while to find the courage to strip off the last layer. I woke up during the night when I stretched my legs to find the bottom of my sleeping bag unpleasantly icy and damp. I must say that it has been a wonderful sleeping bag: I am still sleeping naked while Richard (who is much tougher than I am) is talking about getting his thermals out at night.

We woke to a very welcome sight – Richard had lit another camp fire. Masha had, as usual, forgotten to eat her breakfast oats so we have decided to give her half rations in future. Off at 6.30am, and it was very cold and misty. My new boots (bought in Gdansk), although very comfortable and big enough to wear two pairs of socks, are far from waterproof and my feet were soaking wet and cold all morning.

We were able to follow tracks for a while, then we had to go alongside the railway line. Richard couldn't get through so we agreed to meet at the level crossing near (I thought) to the station at Bialy Bor, where we had been told about another stud. The ride was really rather scary, there was a very faint track most of the way, but we had to keep skirting bogs and fallen trees. Because it was still foggy we didn't dare stray too far from the railway. The horses were marvellous; going through ditches, jumping drains, walking on the very edge of the railway. After jumping one drain, Pompeii stopped dead with his head held to the right. I tried to turn him left, to no avail, and then realized that he had jumped into a tree and had a branch wedged in his bridle, effectively immobilizing him – bless him he didn't panic at all. This really brought home to me the difference between these tough and sensible cookies and, for example, my thoroughbred at home, who would have panicked at least a hundred times by now. The walkie-talkie ran out of battery after a while and we think Richard must have got very worried, but we found each other in the end and Richard gave me a charged battery.

We then separated again because Richard could not get past a barrier, and we agreed to meet at Bialy Bor station. Immediately after passing the barrier, we passed a tiny halt with an unpronounceable name, and then there was a lovely track alongside the railway. I started to worry when the sun struggled through – we were going east. No response from Richard when I called him on the radio. After half an hour so we decided something was wrong, so trotted back. Eventually I made contact with Richard, and discovered that the tiny halt we had passed was Bialy Bor station. The walkie-talkie ran out again (it had not been a fully-charged battery), and Katie and I felt very stupid.

Off to the stables. They had been alerted to our arrival by Krzysztof and we were to stay at a local *pension*. After all the messing around and getting lost, we decided to spend just a couple of hours at Bialy Bor to feed and rest horses, wash our clothes and bodies, and ring Giles. Richard pointed out that if we stayed the night we would never be able to leave at 6am.

We found the stables. They had eighty stallions there and I was told it was a military establishment – we noticed some wonderful, and huge, cross-country jumps. After we had settled the horses, we then found a *pension*, where we washed selves and knickers in the shower and rang Giles. Unfortunately, he had no news about crossing at Szczecin as Bernard van Goethem is away. Then Richard pointed out it was gone 2pm and we might as well stay the night.

30 October – DAY 95
We set off for the stables, where I met a very nice old military chap, Josef, with whom I spoke in Russian. He became quite an admirer – he even discovered I spoke French, which was such a relief after trying to speak German. He showed us the stable's

collection of carriages and kissed my hand twice when we left. Katie was outraged.

Incidentally, he thinks we can cross with horses at one of the Szcezcin borders.

We left at 8am, and made very good progress in the morning, but after lunch we couldn't find the track Richard wanted so we didn't do so well.

31 October – DAY 96
It had to happen some time: while trying to find a track, poor Richard got bogged down; we collected wood to help him, and he was soon clear. Katie was amazed that he remained so good-humoured – I hadn't the heart to point out he was being Action Man for her benefit!

After lunch Richard told us to turn right at the end of the village and head through the forest to a village called Brusno and wait for him there while he went to change some dollars (this was urgent as we had no zloties left and needed some supplies). We did get there eventually (after a great deal of agonizing about which track to take when it forked) and waited in a bitterly cold wind. Forty minutes later he turned up. In future we must ask him to give us a map and some idea of the distance to our rendezvous, and to tell us roughly how long he expects to be.

Not a satisfactory day, although Richard found a reasonably sheltered campsite, and we have a lovely camp fire.

1 November – DAY 97
It was wet and windy all night, reminiscent of our first night in Belarus, only not quite so bad because this site was more sheltered. Woke at 1.30am, and thought about crossing Germany. I have decided that if we can cross near Szcezcin and if I (or Giles or Angelika) can find a German to ride with me and work out a route with stables and accommodation for riders along the way, then I shall definitely finish the ride as planned. If not, then I shall have to accept that a cop-out is necessary and box them all the way to Hamburg.

Off just after 7am. We had to follow roads for a bit, then forest tracks, in one of which the truck got bogged for over four hours! First I helped, getting branches and leafy twigs (and damaged my hand in the process). I then took Pompeii and tried to find somebody with a tractor, but without his women, he behaved disgracefully – bucking and nearly rearing on the road when any traffic passed, so after trying a couple of houses without success, I returned.

By that time Katie was driving, with Richard labouring, so I kept an eye on the horses. Eventually they succeeded in getting the truck out.

All this time the wind howled and the rain was almost horizontal: really very unpleasant. The sun broke through briefly while the Toyota was being extricated from the mud, and in the unaccustomed dryness, Pompeii lay down to roll. The problem was that I was still in the saddle, but when I shouted at him, bless him, he got up immediately. (Richard pointed out later that this proved how light I am). I then took his saddle off and he rolled at once, so I also took Muffin's off and she did likewise. Unfortunately it was a short respite – soon afterwards the rain re-established supremacy.

At my request, Richard searched for and found a Polish farmer with some spare stables, and the horses were warm and dry (albeit tied up) for the night. Pompeii was separated from the mares, which worried me at first, but after a few loud whinnies, he settled down to eat.

The farmer lent us what he called a flat, which consisted of a freezing sitting-room (with a sofa-bed for Katie and me, while Richard had to make do with a mattress on the floor) and a tiny kitchen with running water. Richard cooked some delicious chilli con carne and we had some vodka to warm ourselves up.

2 November – DAY 98

Off at 8.05am, weather now dry (except for a few tiny showers), but even colder than yesterday. Richard managed to find some tracks, and we made good time. This was followed by roadwork, but it was not too bad because there was either a verge or roadside field for quite a lot of the way.

Into Lobez, where Richard had found the stud recommended by Krzysztof and prepared them for our arrival. The two mares were tethered in good stalls, Pompeii, as stallion, had the luxury of a loosebox.

We met the director, Grzegorsz Majewski, who was very kind, welcoming and luckily spoke English. We also met a young man called Tomek who is organizing the catering, and the barman who only speaks German. We had some vodka followed by a delicious meal.

Apparently there is a foxhunt 'Hubertus' tomorrow, organized for the benefit of some Belgians, and we are invited.

Richard is determined I shall not ride across Germany. Even here we get conflicting stories – one chap called Marek told us the border had been closed to horses since May, but Grzegorsz said some horses had come through into Poland only three weeks ago.

3 November – DAY 99

Last night was quite fun, although the Belgians are an awfully rowdy crowd.

Gave up trying to sleep at about 6am, so had a shower and got dressed. I couldn't open the front door so, feeling very stupid, I had to wait for the staff to leave. It seems brute force is required to get the door open. I then found I could not get back into the barracks, so went to the dining room (in another building) for coffee, but everything was locked – I was too early. Went to check the horses, who were fine. I could not find the key to the tack room so I was unable to get my Musto riding coat out to mend it. It was ripped when a couple of drunken Poles tried to pull me out of the saddle. I did have my car keys, so got into the Toyota, only to discover my keys do not fit the ignition, so I looked through all my documents and froze.

Giles rang – he wants me to go through Sweden after all as he is afraid of my using German roads. He has discovered there is a ferry from Swinoujscie to Ystad daily at 1pm.

Richard had the key to the tack room, so we got out the Musto and stuck the torn parts together. Katie and I were in the stables by 10.30am, and were allocated a stallion each. I wore the Musto and, at Grzegorsz's request, my Russian hat. After a frosty start, it started raining as we set off.

It transpires that 'Hubertus' is not fox-hunting, nor even drag-hunting, but consists of following a trail, through the beautiful forest, marked with red ribbons. There are two routes – one for those riders who want to jump, and one for those who do not wish to meet any obstacles. These obstacles are man-made jumps, and are not very large.

Unfortunately, our horses – especially Katie's – had no brakes. Jumping was a nightmare as everyone bunched together and I won't jump if I can't see. Apart from anything else, I really do not think I, riding a stallion, want to crash into another stallion. Luckily, these horses all jump very well so we had no problems actually getting over the fences. Katie and I both got very hot and tired, although by noon it was snowing. Indeed, our struggles with our mounts were such that we did not even dare have a cigarette or a slurp from Katie's hip flask.

At about 2pm we had a break for barbecue and vodka, (I recommend the mixture after rain), and all the riders huddled round a really huge camp fire while the grooms walked the horses around. We then rode back to the stables, where there was a lot of completely mad galloping around chasing the 'fox' (a man wearing a brush on his shoulder), which I nearly caught.

More booze, then rang Giles. He is very keen that I should ride as far as possible, so I explained about the snowstorm (and the weather is hardly likely to improve much as the days draw in and we head even further north). I therefore asked him if he could please try to get a contact in the Swedish riding network so we could find stables for some nights if the weather was truly awful. The latest decision is to ride nearly to Swinoujscie, then box the horses from that port over to Ystad in Sweden.

CHAPTER TWELVE

Frustrations in Western Poland

5 November – DAY 100

The night before last we had a party, which was quite fun although these Belgians are extremely noisy. To my huge embarrassment, Grzegorsz proposed a toast to me, and everybody joined in the 'hip, hip, hurrah!' and said how brave I was. Richard and I (Katie had gone to bed, exhausted) were able for the first time to see our own video. It was a bit difficult (and rather embarrassing) with everyone else watching it too, and for some reason there was no sound, but we think it should produce something quite good, when edited.

The most energetic dancer was Tomac, who is a vet and a jump judge, but assured me solemnly he was too old to jump himself – at fifty. I told him what rubbish that was, and that I was nearly fifty myself. 'Ah, but you are young', he told me. I think he is gay – which is a pity because he is really rather good looking. When we parted, he kissed me the Polish way (three times) and said he liked me very, very much.

I think I have reached such a state of sexual frustration that I find far more men attractive than I normally do. If this journey lasts much longer, I fear I shall get to a situation when I fancy anything in trousers.

Today I discovered something interesting: the Polish word for 'three-day eventing' is 'military', which of course means that the stud at Bialy Bor was probably nothing to do with the army, and we did see some wonderful cross-country jumps there.

The next day we took Katie to Berlin airport – she has the carrot of the new boyfriend waiting for her, and the stick of having to pay the rent, so we agreed I could ride across Sweden by myself. We had quite a good run (three hours), and the border crossing was surprisingly quick, but it snowed quite heavily for a while.

We then drove into Berlin itself because Richard insists I must have thermals. We parked the Toyota and took a taxi. The shops were all horrendously expensive, and we bought boots, thermal longjohns and Gore-tex gloves. By a miracle, my credit card came up trumps and paid like a little lamb. On leaving, I rang Giles for the first time on the new digital portable Europhone he had brought out to Poland at my suggestion [and what a lifesaver it was later to be].

Today the Belgians left after breakfast and, although they were charming, I must admit it was blissfully quiet thereafter. Richard and I took the horses for a walk, then had a drink before going out for lunch. We found a really good restaurant and ate and drank, and talked happily for about three hours. We then returned to the building which contains the restaurant and took some vodka up to the Germans, who were having a party and drinking in Leshnik's room (Leshnik the 'horse-master').

Leshnik, after drinking a great deal of vodka, announced that he would like to ride with me across Sweden. I told him I would be delighted, but of course he has to get permission from the boss, and privately I doubt he will.

6 November – DAY 101
Another boring day. I sent a fax to the Polish veterinary authorities, and went to see Grzegorsz. I asked him about the Health Certificate, which we needed a vet to fill in and sign. Having exported horses to the EC himself, he knew exactly what I wanted, but assured me that this paper was not necessary to get into Sweden because we would only be in transit. I was doubtful, but he repeated his assurances that this certificate would not be necessary until we got to our final destination – England.

Grzegorsz has found two places for us to stay as I ride to the ferry, one house belonging to some English language teachers called George and Alice, which is in a tiny place called Imno, and a farm run by a woman called Veronica. The plan is that we spend Wednesday night at Imno and Thursday night with Veronica, and another contact of Grzegorsz (yet another Belgian, called Victor) has promised to take the horses in his box to Ystad.

Supper in town. Richard and I have found a wonderful restaurant with delicious food and very reasonable prices. Now that we are alone (and I am not riding) we are becoming much more, I want to use the word intimate, although that implies a relationship we do not have. I am now getting his side of the story of the tension between him and Ali. One example is the episode of locking the keys in the truck. He admits it was careless of him, but points out that due to his fear of doing just that, he had given a spare set to Ali, never dreaming she would leave the keys in her jacket in the cab. He has also apologized: 'I am sorry if the tension between Ali and me ruined your expedition.' I also learned a bit about Richard's past, and was amazed to discover that he spoke Farsi (which he learned as part of a military mission to Persia some years ago).

7 November – DAY 102

We found the ferry terminal and the offices, and booked the horse box and the Toyota for the sailing on Friday. We had asked the Polish laboratory to post the results of the blood tests they were analyzing to the ferry office at Swinoujscie (because we are 'of no fixed abode'), but there was no letter from them.

On our return journey we looked for and eventually found Imno and found Grzegorsz's friends, George and Alice, who were both incredibly charming and welcoming. In addition to teaching English in Szcezcin they also breed Shetland ponies. They explained that they would not be there to greet us tomorrow because Alice has to go into hospital, but introduced us to Asha, a very attractive, but rather tense woman in her thirties, who helps them with the horses. She was very worried because she does not speak English, but we reassured her (via George) that we would have two Polish girls with us.

8 November – DAY 103

An excellent riding day. We tacked up and Grzegorsz arrived with Edita and her friend, Yola who had offered to ride with me as far as Swinoujscie. We covered over fifty kilometres (thirty miles), even though we didn't leave until after 8.30am. A couple of grooms from the stud showed us the way through the forest.

The horses are in fine fettle after their long rest. The weather has been glorious but very cold – in sheltered places the frost lingered all day. Yet again I have to record that these Polish forests are stunningly beautiful. We saw a lot of deer, probably more today than in the whole of the trip so far.

Arrived at Imno just before it got dark – the horses had been allocated different stables, but they were fine. Pompeii neighed loudly for ages because he was separated from his mares and could not see them – since they did not deign to answer his neighs, he never found out that they were right next door.

To my surprise, a strange man was there to greet us and it turned out he is a journalist, also called Richard. He took a lot of photographs as we arrived and untacked.

9 November – DAY 104

Woke at 7am and went to the guest house, where I had coffee with Richard.

I returned to the house to get the girls up and found Richard (the journalist) and George, who had got home last night after we had gone to sleep, waiting to interview me for the paper. Richard kept pushing for sensational stories and was obviously disappointed by my rather tame account of my venture. In the end I said that the point was not the reality of the danger, but that the danger had been an ever-present possibility and I had faced it and, as it so often happens, once faced, it never materialized.

George then suggested that, for the sake of twenty kilometres, we should stay here instead of going on to Veronica – who in any case had never been contacted and we did not even know if there would be anyone there when we arrived. I discussed this with Richard who agreed, and we spoke to the girls, who were very relieved.

Then I had to get the horses out, tack up Pompeii and let Richard take a whole load of photographs. Pompeii continues to shout for the mares, but they don't answer so he still doesn't know they are right next door.

Just before noon Richard took the girls back to Lobez. While he was gone, I tried to make polite conversation with Asha, and it turns out her Russian, although rusty, is quite good enough for us to communicate. After his return, we drove to Veronica's where Richard is to meet Vincent at 7.30am tomorrow morning. She spoke only German, but was very welcoming and insisted on giving us coffee. We then had supper in a transport café and I rang Sirvi in Sweden to let her know our time of arrival. She has found some stables (with some difficulty, as she knows nothing about horses and neither do any of her friends) and has said we can stay in her flat near Ystad. [NB: Sirvi Rasberg is an old friend of Giles's.]

CHAPTER THIRTEEN

Fighting the Swedish Bureaucrats

10 November – DAY 105

We got up at 6am and Richard drove to Veronica's to meet Vincent as planned but, in spite of the arrangements we had made, Vincent turned up at Imno. George had never returned, so we all hope there is nothing wrong with Alice (whose operation, I gathered from Asha, was on one of her eyes). I left him a thank you note.

Richard reappeared, having sensibly realized what was going on, and we loaded the horses. Considering they had never in their lives been in a horsebox before, they were angelic (Pompeii led the way, as usual). I was very nervous because the ramp was rickety, and extremely rotten and dangerous – Vincent nearly put his foot through it when he went in to spread some straw. I went with the horses to the port, and had to keep asking Vincent to slow down and not to use his hands conversationally when driving. Joking apart, it was a nightmare ride as I really do not want these horses ruined by their first-ever experience of motorized transport. We stopped once or twice to check them, and, although they were all being good and quiet, poor Pompeii must have been really frightened as he had worked himself up into a sweat.

At last we arrived at the port and luckily the weather was dead calm and actually foggy. There was a last-minute panic because we couldn't find the vet who was supposed to be on duty to sign our papers. Grzegorsz magically appeared and helped, and we got out with some sort of paper.

We had an excellent crossing but we arrived in Ystad (7.30pm) to a complete nightmare. Waiting for us were about twenty journalists, but no vet. The journalists, however, were very kind and helpful, and one of them tried to help me get hold of the officials I needed. They were amazed at my journey.

Thanks to their intervention, a vet was summoned, and arrived two hours later. He was very nice, but terribly wet. He finally announced he could not let us through because the horse passports (Russian) did not adequately identify the horses. I could see his point (they only give the name and colour), but why had nobody told me before I left that this would be a problem? Surely some of the officials in the EC must know that this is a difficulty with Russian passports?

Sadly, my long-suffering horses had to go into quarantine. They behaved impeccably – standing quietly in the box for four hours on the quayside before being sealed in by Customs and taken off by Victor to the quarantine stables about seventy kilometres away, by which time they will have spent over fourteen hours in their first-ever horse-box. We followed Sirvi back to her flat in Simrishamn, getting home around midnight.

11 November – DAY 106

Quiet day. We watched our video for the first time in peace and with sound. I was rung by BBC Radio 5, who said they want to interview me tomorrow at 7.45am Swedish time for a live news broadcast – help! Still, nobody I know is likely to be listening to any radio station at 6.45am on a Sunday.

The local papers are full of my journey, most of them describing me as 'potty'. The only quote I truly value (having asked Giles to translate for me) was 'Barbara is an adventuress worthy of the name' – I am really proud of that one.

We took Sirvi out for supper to one of her recommended local restaurants, where we had a delicious meal. The waitress said 'Excuse me, but weren't you in the papers today?' Fame at last!

12 November – DAY 107

Woke early in a panic about the interview. Richard brought me coffee at 7.30am. I was literally shaking with fear while I hung on the phone waiting for the interview. Giles said later I sounded very composed. Apparently I said I sent the Cossacks back to England, but Brian Hayes, the interviewer, did not notice and instead made much of the fact that I said the horses were very philosophical.

Sirvi is going out to lunch with Ebbe, her estranged husband, and their son, Martin. It is Father's Day here, and apparently by Swedish tradition it is a day for all the family. Richard and I went off to find the horses. The directions given by Sirvi's friend would have been perfect, but they were directions from Malmö and not from Simrishamn. We found the farm in the end, but the cagey owner (Bertil Zaar) would not let us see the horses because they are in quarantine. Before departing we left all our documents with him (having got a receipt), so that the local vet could pick them up and inspect them later. I have been told that blood samples were taken yesterday.

I spoke to the local official vet (Hans Andren) at great length on my mobile phone, which works here. He seemed quite Swedishly official and burbled on for ages (my poor phone bill) basically justifying the Swedish attitude. One problem apart from identification seems to be the Russian veterinary certificates, which nobody can read. I asked what diseases did the EC fear, other than the ones the horses have been repeatedly tested for. None. 'So what is the problem?' I asked. 'Do you care if they were riddled with disease when we left, as long as they are healthy now?' That stumped him.

We went into Malmö to look around and then decided to have a pizza. The owner of the restaurant we chose was of Middle-Eastern appearance, and the cook spoke very little English. While we were eating, I heard the cook speaking on the telephone in something very like Russian, yet not Russian. When he brought coffee I thanked him in Russian. He automatically said '*Pazhalsta*' (thank you) before doing a double take. We chatted for a while in Russian, and it transpired that he is Bulgarian. He told us the owner of the restaurant was Iranian, so Richard could have spoken to him in Farsi – an unlikely double for two Brits in a Swedish town.

After lunch we rang Dr Andren again. He had seen my papers and was still quibbling, but seemed slightly more positive and helpful. I am to ring the Swedish Board of Agriculture in the morning.

On our return to Simrishamn we found Sirvi very upset because Ebbe had done his duty on Father's Day, but with very bad grace – she says he has a new woman. I told her to forget him and not see him if that is how he is going to behave. 'But I need him,' she said, with tears in her eyes. 'What for?' It turned out that she depends on him for D.I.Y. in her new flat. We said we could do a lot and told her that she must use her friends more.

We all had lots of vodka, Sirvi cheered up, Richard finished the cooking and did the washing up, during which time Sirvi confided she was very worried about Richard because she is so fond of Giles, and I suddenly realized she thinks we are altogether too friendly. I hastened to reassure her. Richard and I even agreed to talk to her English class tomorrow.

13 November – DAY 108

I had a dreadfully frustrating time on the phone to the Swedish Board of Agriculture. After several attempts I got through to the bigwig Giles had sent a fax to earlier, Bengt Nordblom, who was very nice and seemed keen to help, but had passed everything to Dr Karin Cerenius. After a long chat, he told me he was a cavalry man and knew what it is like to spend hours and days in the saddle, and that it must all have been very interesting. Indeed it had, I assured him.

Sirvi rang to say that the time she had given us for her English class was one hour later than it should have been, so we had to rush over to the school. We spoke to the children and showed a bit of our video.

Back to phone the Agriculture people at Jönköping, but Dr Cerenius was still unavailable, so I tried Dr Andren, who asked me to call back in half an hour. When I did so, he told me they were still discussing me and my horses, and that someone would ring me on Sirvi's line. In the meantime, I tried Bernard van Goethem and was given another number, on which I finally got through. He was very nice, but basically said he was leaving it to the Swedes to sort out with the ever-helpful Bob Davies at the Ministry of Agriculture, Fisheries and Food, but that if I had any problems, not to hesitate to let him know. As usual, nobody from Jönköping ever rang me back.

14 November – DAY 109

Yet another frustrating day: I stayed by the phone in case any of the Board of Agriculture people rang, but they didn't. Endless calls by me, leaving messages, resulted in a call back at about 6pm to say all OK! Great, I thought. 'You can take your horses through Sweden to Gothenburg on a lorry.'

Oh, shit!

Shall go to Jönköping tomorrow, confront the pompous sods without notice, and suggest someone rides with me to ensure that I do not contaminate any of their precious equines. I am not going to give up tamely.

15 November – DAY 110

Ghastly. Woke at 2am, couldn't get back to sleep, so got up at 3am and made tea and read Russian (I am now in a panic because Giles is trying to get me a job as a Russian interpreter). Unfortunately, I woke Richard, so we left at 4.50am after breakfast to drive the 200 kilometres (124 miles) to Jönköping. Nordblom didn't want to see me, and passed the buck to Karin Cerenius. She didn't ring back (as usual) so I rang her. She tried to fob me off with a minion, but I told her that Nordblom had said I should see her – 2pm she said.

We had no idea of the way to the Board of Agriculture, so we hailed a taxi which led us there. We were a bit early, so we waited. We then had to wait some more, and it was after 2.30pm when we were taken up. Karin Cerenius and Annica Wallen Norell were adamant, and I had to bow to the inevitable – the horses are to travel in a sealed box to Gothenburg. I was really depressed on the way home, and Richard tried to cheer me up. Sirvi cooked a delicious meal and I was in bed by 10.30pm.

16 November – DAY 111

Am in a state of shock – the quarantine costs SEK325 per horse per day plus 25 percent tax. That is a total of about £120 per day. I am worried about money, about weather from Gothenburg, about the horses' welfare now (I am still not allowed to see them) and on the journey. I am getting quotes for transporting them via Gothenburg and via Holland, but how long does it take and will the Germans and/or Dutch let them through?

I am seriously tempted to rush them back to Poland immediately and ask Vincent how much he would charge to keep them for a month under veterinary supervision, after which they could be boxed home, or for three months (with the last month under veterinary supervision) so I could ride them home in March.

One of my problems is that for various reasons the Swedes really do not want to know about me and my horses. They are new to the EC and terrified of letting some feared disease into the Community, I have now been told that they are an exceptionally bureaucratic race, and, to cap it all, there is an outbreak of something called 'Newcastle disease', which affects all birds and is causing thousands of farmyard fowl to be slaughtered. Fortunately, they are kind enough not to blame me for this pestilence.

17 November – DAY 112
After spending literally hours telephoning Swedish and English horse transport companies, I have decided to get the Curragh Bloodstock people to come and fetch the horses because they have a box which is going back empty after delivering some horses to somewhere in Scandinavia. How much will it cost? How much money am I going to need? Have I got enough? Can Giles send me some more? Dare I ask for more – he has spent so much already.

After all these phone calls I have a new worry. All the Swedish companies have told me that sailing from Gothenburg at this time of the year could cause a problem – the sea might be too rough for the horses (bearing in mind they are unable to vomit) – and we would simply not be allowed to take them on board, or it might start out calm but the sea might be much rougher once we got out to the middle of the North Sea. Apart from my very real concern for the horses' welfare while travelling, what happens if they are not allowed to board the ferry? The horsebox is sealed, as in effect the poor things are still in quarantine, so where could we stable them while we waited for the weather to calm down?

I rang Annica Wallen Norell, who seems to be in charge of my case and, when I finally got through to her, I asked her if she could please change the letter of authority permitting me to leave Sweden and to state that I may leave from Malmö instead of from Gothenburg. She did agree, with rather bad grace, after I had pointed out that my request was made on the urging of the Swedish transport companies and that I was rather surprised that none of the vets in Sweden seemed to have spared a thought for the welfare of my horses.

From Malmö we can drive down through Denmark, then there is another short sea-crossing to Germany.

I have rung the British Embassy and complained about the costs of the quarantine and the general lack of co-operation by the Swedish authorities. Unfortunately, there is nothing they can do, but they did make sympathetic noises.

18 November – DAY 113
Yet another frustrating day. I am having to juggle with the various costs – obviously the charges at the quarantine stables are little short of crippling, but transport costs are also expensive, and it will be much cheaper if we can ship our horses home in a lorry that is on a return journey to England, which means we have to fit in with the outward trip. More problems.

22 November – DAY 117
Everything is ready to go tomorrow. I have heard from the driver of the Curragh horsebox, a Norwegian called Thorleif, and we have agreed to meet at the port of Trelleborg because Richard and I have to go there to guide a customs official to the quarantine stables so that the horsebox can be officially sealed, and because Thorleif knows the port well.

Richard has also been to see the local excise people, who have told him that we do not have to pay the 25 percent tax on the quarantine costs, to my great relief. Bertil Zaar is being extraordinarily stubborn, though, and refused to accept this ruling until Giles faxed through a copy of a VAT demand form to show that he is registered.

Richard and I have seen the customs officials at Ystad, because we need a form (of course). They told us we could not have this essential form without a 'transit paper', obtainable only from the freight-forwarding agents. These agents will not issue a transit form because this is a situation which is not 'in the book'. The customs officials do not know what to do. They are completely hopeless and totally flummoxed by this situation, because there is nothing in their rules and regulations (or whatever Bible they live by) to tell them what to do.

While the customs wimps thought about my problem, Richard and I went off to get the cash that Giles had so brilliantly been able to send via Western Union. Another trail of incompetence – the WU agency that I had been told had the cash turned out to be a filling station, and the staff there had never heard of Western Union. I rang Giles, who rang the WU agents in Cambridge. 'Oh, sorry, did we tell you to go there? Never mind, try the ferry terminal'. We returned to the ferry terminal, 'Sorry, we know nothing about any money from England. Try the foreign exchange desk'. The foreign exchange desk, it goes without saying, was closed. Hours later and even angrier, we did eventually get the money.

Back to the customs office, where at last I found an official with a spark of intelligence and a willingness to flirt. Suddenly a solution was found – we could have our essential document if we agreed to pay a 'bond' which these people assure me will be returned once we are in England. 'Fine', I said, 'how much?' 'How much were the horses?' 'One million Russian roubles each', I said – which was no help to the Swedes. I regret to say that I have become so incompetent myself I told them that a million roubles was £400, and was about to be stuck with a bill for £600 for all three horses. I came to my senses just in time – one million roubles is about £140, so the amount we had to pay was about £200.

23 November – DAY 118

Richard and I were all ready to leave at 5pm when I had a call from Annica at 4.30pm – we would not be allowed to depart because she had telephoned her opposite number in Germany to warn him of our arrival (why?) and he had panicked. We are not to be allowed to take the horses through Germany.

What next? How and when am I ever going to get out of this hateful bloody bureaucratic country? I could cheerfully take a bomb and throw it at those smug bastards at Jönköping.

A bomb not being readily available, I did the next best thing and rang Bernard van Goethem in Brussels. He and his colleague, Dietrich Russow, seemed to be appalled at the way I have been treated. The Swedes could have let us in on a temporary permit, the Poles should have issued a proper Health Certificate, and the Germans had no reason whatsoever not to let the horses through in a sealed box. Eventually, Brussels decreed that the blood samples which were taken when we arrived should now be analyzed (why the hell were they not analyzed earlier?) and, if they prove negative, we can be given official documents, which leave us clear to travel freely anywhere in the EEC.

Meanwhile, who pays the extra cost of quarantine? The horsebox was by this time waiting at Trelleborg – who pays the extra cost of that? It seems clear to me that we have spent at least ten days or a fortnight here quite unnecessarily.

Annica has graciously agreed to the instructions from Brussels, and has told me it will only take two or three days to test the blood.

After sorting that lot out, Richard and I had to leap in the truck and drive to Trelleborg, where we met up with Thorleif. He was amazingly relaxed about being told that, far from taking the ferry from Malmö tonight, we just might, with a lot of luck and if the Gods are feeling really kind, be allowed to leave on Monday. 'OK' he said.

24 November – DAY 119

I rang Annica to find out what time I could leave on Monday (assuming the blood samples would test negative) – that is to say, I spent most of the morning trying to make contact. When I first rang, she was out (nothing new there), and then for four hours I was unable to get through to the main switchboard. I need hardly have bothered – when I did speak to her she was extremely unhelpful. The results should be through over the weekend, and then the official vet could sign the certificates. 'What time on Monday could we expect to go?' I asked. 'We are as anxious to leave as you must be to get rid of us.' 'When the papers are signed by the vet – I cannot order him to do it, you know.'

Have had several conversations with a woman called Jessica from the *Daily Telegraph*. She had said she wanted to meet me in Copenhagen (that being the closest town with a large international airport) to do a thorough interview. She rang this morning to say she was ill, which was quite a relief really as I am not sure how much the journey to Copenhagen would have cost, nor how expensive the hotels are.

25 November – DAY 110
Richard having returned to Poland for the weekend (poor man, although he has done masses of useful things for Sirvi, like hanging pictures and putting up shelves), is going mad with boredom here. Sirvi took me sightseeing in the morning. One of the sights was the beautiful beach where everyone went to bathe and sunbathe in the summer – it would have been a really lovely beach to ride along – but of course Sirvi thought 'it is not allowed to ride on Swedish beaches'.

Sweden has something in common with England – every village, however tiny, has a beautiful church but there are now not enough people to fill it.

In the evening Thorleif rang. 'Is it true we are going on Wednesday?' Where did he hear that? With any luck we will be arriving in England on Wednesday. He also mentioned that at the house of some friends in Malmö he had met Elizabeth Swensson, the local Official Vet, who had never heard of me or my horses. Why not?

26 November – DAY 111
Woke in a sweat after nightmares about ferries, vets and documents. Will we ever get away? Sirvi (who is not Swedish-born but from Estonia, although she has lived here since she was a small child) is predicting that we will still be here at Christmas and is urging me to do all my Christmas shopping.

I went to church and the service was predictably boring because I could not understand it, although there was plenty of singing. Two babies were christened, oddly, in the middle of the service. The interior decor was fascinating, it was as though a Swede had decorated it (all very tasteful in white and grey) and then, as soon as his back was turned, a mad Russian – or even Mongolian – had rushed in and installed the pulpit. This had a three-quarter life-size saint as the pillar, and a positively Oriental clash of red, black, and gold on the pulpit itself, the whole surmounted by an equally lurid roof suspended from the ceiling. There were also three or four large replicas of ships hanging from the ceiling – I suppose that can be accounted for by the fact that Simrishamn has been a port for centuries.

I rang to book the ferry – on Thorleif's recommendation we are not going from Malmö but from Trelleborg to Travemunde in

Germany. The transaction was quite straightforward except they asked me the years that Richard and I were born. I was intrigued, and asked why. Could it be that only people over or under the age of, say, forty were allowed to cross from Trelleborg to Travemunde? Maybe only teenagers were permitted to travel on Mondays? The answer was far more prosaic and sad. 'Since the *Estonia* ferry sank, the rule-loving Swedes had decided it was necessary to know the ages of all passengers, so that in a crisis, the elderly could be located and helped to safety.'

27 November – DAY 112
Rang Elizabeth Swensson, the Official Vet, who was very kind and helpful but is mystified as to why she has heard nothing about us as the main part of her job is signing health certificates for horses! She did say that she found it impossible to work with Lars Lund, who has taken over from Hans Andren as the local vet.

Rang Annica – the horses' blood samples have tested negative. She will fax a new directive to Lund, and I also rang him to give him some essential information. Bernard van Goethem assures me that no other document is necessary beyond what the Swedes are preparing, as long as we stay in the EC. 'I assure you that after this experience there is no way I would even think of leaving the EC and trying to come in again,' I told him.

We told the customs office in Ystad that it was no longer necessary for one of their officials to seal the horse box. I was unsurprised when they informed me that they had not heard from Annica to that effect, so I had to ring her again and ask her to let customs know that everything was now in order.

At last we set off to fetch my horses. We had agreed to meet Thorleif at the nearest motorway exit, and were waiting for him there when he rang me – he had decided to continue and was now in the next town. Eventually we found each other and we led him to the quarantine stables. After we had handed over the outrageous sum of over £1,600 for seventeen days' quarantine, the horses were led out. We were not permitted to go into the stables and fetch them, and when I saw the horses I understood why – they were in much poorer condition than they had been when they arrived. Thorleif warned me not to say anything, adding that he had seen this situation a hundred times and that there was nothing we could do about it. At the price charged I had every right to expect them to have been fed like royalty and groomed by handmaidens on a daily basis.

Please, God, let everything be all right.

Later
Everything is fine. We boarded the ferry at Trelleborg with no problems at all, and I am now in a very smart and spacious cabin after a delicious dinner. Thank you, God.

28 November – DAY 113

Woke after yet more nightmares, this time because Giles has said there will be a lot of reporters at Harwich. How on earth will I cope with reporters and (apparently) television cameras, when I fall apart just giving a radio interview?

Had breakfast with Richard and Thorleif, and we rejoined our vehicles. After driving off the ferry, we debated whether to wait for Thorleif and the horses. There being nowhere obviously suitable to wait, we drove on through Northern Germany until we got to the first motorway service station, where we parked the Toyota and waited. An hour later, trying not to worry, it suddenly occurred to me that the port authorities may well have let the horsebox off first so as not to subject the horses to the fumes of a hundred engines. Since Thorleif had my mobile number and had not made contact, I decided firmly to stop worrying and we drove off.

When we were finally reunited with the horse box at The Hook of Holland, Thorleif told us that the German authorities at Travemunde had held him up for three hours, in spite of the fact that Thorleif had dozens of documents to show that everything was in order. In the end they sealed up the box and reluctantly let him go.

Giles rang to say that my story and photographs (from my hunting expedition two years earlier) were splashed over almost every national paper in England. In fits of giggles, he quoted a headline about 'Incredible journey at 2,500 miles per stallion'. Apparently the papers had just finished with a much-reported television interview with Princess Diana and a gruesome murder trial, and were short of a human interest story. Some of the tabloids had given me a whole page, with maps of our route and so on.

The rest of the day was a mixture of dream and nightmare. ITN rang to interview me for their lunchtime news (on which Giles was to appear with Julia Somerville, to his great joy), the *Daily Express* and the *Daily Mail* reporters were ringing at frequent intervals and ended up trying to outbid each other for an exclusive – at which point I sicked them onto Giles who, being as he himself admitted, a child in these matters, promptly sicked them on to Vivienne Schuster, my literary agent. [It was the best move he ever made, he told me later.]

Thanks to the glories of modern technology ('Richard', I begged, 'please take me back to Russia!'), I was able to meet at a service station the *Daily Express* team, who had actually taken the trouble to come to Germany. Since at that stage I thought the *Mail* was getting the exclusive, I was pretty noncommittal, but by the time we got to The Hook of Holland, the boot was on the other foot and I had been 'bought' by the *Express*. The *Daily Mail* team was at the ferry terminal at the Hook, so now I had to avoid them.

Eventually the *Express* team bought our tickets and smuggled us on board, where we (including Thorleif) had a really delicious dinner courtesy of that newspaper before retreating to our cabins.

29 November – DAY 114
I really do not know what plane, I am on. We arrived at Harwich to the expected hordes of reporters and television crews. I gave what I suppose must be called a brief press conference before the *Express* team whisked me away in Giles's car. Those poor waiting journalists were not even allowed a glimpse of the horses, who remained in the box. They were not going to give up easily, however, and those few who did not follow us followed the horsebox, which now contained Ali, as well as Thorleif and the horses.

I found this worrying; Giles and I had thought that there would be a short photo opportunity for all the press, TV cameras and so on, with the in-depth interviews reserved for our new 'owners'. However, this was changed at the last minute and all photo access to the horses was denied. We felt truly sorry for the cameramen, some of whom had come 200 miles to no purpose. Still, as the man from the *Express* said, 'Yes, but if they owned you, they'd be doing it to us!'

We all met up at the house of William, a friend of Ali's, who had agreed to let us (and the horses) stay the night, although when the arrangement was made we were expecting to arrive there in the saddle. Dozens of reporters almost came to blows and tried to force their way on to William's property. They were all disappointed – the only sight they got of the horses was from a distance. In the meantime, the *Express* got a million snaps of me with the horses, me with Giles, the horses bucking as they were released into the field, the horses rolling, and so on.

I wanted to *ride* to William's place.

For about two hours in the afternoon I told my story to Richard, the *Express* journalist, and then in the evening we all went to the Swan Hotel at Lavenham, where we had a really scrumptious meal and spent the night. But before I was allowed to go to bed, I had to spend another two hours telling the rest of my story.

30 November – DAY 115

The *Express* team had firmly announced I would not be allowed to ride the rest of the way home, but by this time I had had enough of being pushed around and put my foot down – they had denied me one day's ride, I simply would not hear of them denying me the very last leg. We returned to William's before dawn, caught the horses (with some difficulty – they were enjoying their new-found freedom), tacked them up and Ali and I rode them across farm tracks to the road. We could not simply leave by the main entrance because there was a reporter lurking in the village who subsequently spent most of the morning chasing Giles's car all over Essex.

We spent the rest of the day – my last of the trip – trying to dodge reporters, and Ali and I could not believe that we succeeded. I suppose none of them could have known about horses and our speed of progress, because had any of them simply drawn a line between where we started and where we were to finish, that line would have crossed our path a dozen times. How could they have missed us?

I had taken my mobile phone so as to check with Giles on the reporters hanging around in our village. We were about a mile from home when it rang – a man from the Russian newspaper *Izvestia* wanted to talk to me about my journey. His English was not brilliant, so I spoke in Russian and explained that I was still on the horse, so would he please ring me at home in about half an hour. Ali said that was the most extraordinarily evocative moment, in a field of set-aside in the middle of Suffolk, there I was speaking Russian again. So at last my three brave and amazingly untired horses have made it safely from Alexikovo to Denston, and are now snug in my stables, eating their heads off with presumably no idea that our adventures are not to continue tomorrow, or next week. I wonder how long it will take them to realize that they have finally arrived?

Afterthoughts

To my continuing amazement, the media interest persisted for a while. Four days after our return, we appeared on *The Richard and Judy Show*, who insisted on having one of the horses in the studio too. I decided that really Pompeii was the only one laid back enough to risk taking in among all the lights, cameras and (most dangerous of all) cables trailing all over the floor. Ali went up to Liverpool with him in a horsebox, and they stayed in a hotel on the Wirral with stables next door. Ali was staggered to discover that the horse-box driver, Derek, was the very same man who had driven Marek's marsh-ponies from Kuligi to Suffolk! Richard and I flew up from Cambridge. My faith in Pompeii was justified and he slept through the entire interview. Unfortunately, the crew told us that there was not room for Richard and Ali, as well as me and the horse, so they tossed a coin and Ali won.

Naturally, when Selina Scott also asked if I would take a horse to her studio, it was my beloved Pompeii who accompanied me. On that occasion, however, he was required to go in a lift. It was a freight lift, fortunately, very large and slow, but Pompeii was afraid when the lift moved, and it is a tribute to his essential bravery that he did not throw a wobbly and kill us all.

Gradually we settled in – what adaptable creatures we all are. The mares were turned out in a large field where they made themselves instantly at home. I fed them and checked them daily, but they soon reverted to their previously wild state and could not even be touched. We had another example of their incredible common sense after only a few days – Malishka somehow slipped and fell in the very muddy conditions, and got sheep-netting wire between her hoof and her shoe on three of her feet. I got a phone call to come at once, so Giles and I rushed over – it was only about an hour after I had fed them, so at least we knew she hadn't been lying there all night. Now, this is a nightmare scenario. Most horses would have struggled and kicked until they hurt themselves really badly, but Malishka just lay there waiting to be rescued. I knelt by her head and talked to her calmly while Giles, with superhuman strength, struggled and sweated with inadequate wire-cutters – everything hopelessly slippery with mud – until he got her free. She then got up calmly and stood as though nothing had happened! Having caught her, we took this chance to take both mares into the stables and sent for the farrier – an earlier appointment to have their shoes removed had had to be cancelled because I simply couldn't catch them.

Pompeii stayed at our stables for a couple of weeks until he was no longer required to be a television star, then his shoes were removed and he was put out with the mares. I kept riding him until we turned him out, but found it an incredibly odd sensation to go out for a ride and then come back to where we started.

For me, the first few weeks were difficult. I had known it would be hard for me to readapt to normal life, but the strange situation was compounded by the fact that Roy Cutts, who had taken care of everything wonderfully while I was away, had actually reached his retirement birthday while I was still in Poland. Being him, of course, he had carried on working, but now that I was home, he wanted to get some rest and spend more time beating for the local shoots. This meant that on some days I would give a radio or television interview before returning home to put on my wellies and muck out the stables.

When I first returned I looked at my wardrobe and was appalled. Did I really have that many clothes? Surely nobody could need six skirts, several dresses and innumerable pullovers? And why did I have so many jackets? I was ashamed. But now, four months after my return, I find myself browsing through the mail-order catalogues thinking, 'I cannot live another day without that absolutely wonderful pair of trousers'. As I said, we are amazingly adaptable.

Another thing which shocked me deeply on my return was the rampant consumerism. Sitting in the Green Rooms of various commercial television stations, waiting to be interviewed, I was horrified, not just by the number of advertisements but at the sheer uselessness of the items being promoted. Having spent so long with people who have literally only the barest necessities, and having washed my clothes by hand with any kind of soap available, I could not see why three different varieties of fabric conditioner were on offer. Have we in the West all gone mad?

One more point – why do supermarkets have so much food? Why are there ten different varieties of baked beans? Who needs a choice of fifty breakfast cereals? Why are we offered exotic and out-of-season fruit and vegetables? How much unnecessary aviation fuel is burnt up bringing us these treats?

On the subject of food, I did not cook at all until Christmas Day. Giles produced lovely meals from the supermarket shelves, at which I had always previously sneered as being too expensive and an unnecessary luxury. While I struggled to resume normal life, copy my diary on to my computer, muck out and so on, these easy meals were gratefully accepted. I just could not get back into a normal routine, and Giles's catering helped enormously.

Sleeping is still a problem – I am simply unable to sleep in a normal bed. For a long time I slept on the floor, but have returned to my half of the bed by the simple expedient of throwing away the mattress and sleeping on the board that had previously lived under it. This has made me a very easy guest. Once a week I stay with Katie in her flat in London, and all I need is an area of floor to unroll my air mattress and lay my sleeping bag on it.

To return to the horses – towards the beginning of February I realized that Masha was not just fattening up nicely, as I had thought, but was heavily in foal. We decided that even a tough Russian foal would not get the best start in life if it was born in a snow-drift in the middle of the night, so we made arrangements for them to come home. This meant that my beloved, gentle Arab mare, Aysha, had to be sent away to livery, where I may say she is very happy as a companion to an in-foal mare. By giving away the geese, I released a small stable which had been their home; I had a spare stable after finding another home for the goats before I left England, so we were able to accommodate my thorough-bred mare, Isabel, as well as the three Russians. With great cunning, and using the electric fence wire to herd them into a corner, we succeeded in catching the horses and brought them home: not a moment too soon, as three days later, on 2 March, Giles went back to check Masha, a couple of hours after giving the morning haynets, to find a large colt foal. In the space of that two hours, she had given birth, bitten the umbilical cord and cleaned him up. Giles was quite hurt that his years of experience in animal obstetrics were unwanted, but was, of course, over the moon. And where was I? Ironically I was in Germany, visiting Tatiana Myelnikova, who was staying with her parents near Munich.

Malishka, whose stable is next to Masha's, spent the first few days staring at the new arrival with her jaw dropping. Isabel's reaction was the same. We are all very proud of Masha. I had no idea she was in foal, although I should have guessed that she might be when Malishka had her miscarriage. What's more, I think back with even greater horror to the night before we rode through Minsk, when she fell over and we thought she had broken her neck. We could easily had had another miscarriage there.

Like the puppy we found in the bus shelter, the foal has been named Ashibka – it means 'mistake' in Russian, which is not entirely appropriate as 'surprise' would better have described him. There is no doubt in our minds that Pompeii is the sire. Not only is little Shibka (for short) the same colour, but he also has the same bold manner and an attitude that you are there for his convenience, not the other way about.

Sadly, both the mares must be sold. I bought them in order to sell them to endurance riders who would continue to prove the point I think I have already made. Pompeii, I am determined to keep – I really love him and he was a Christmas present. I know it will not be easy, keeping him away from in-season mares is a continuing problem, and next spring I shall be off on my travels again. Mongolia to Germany (Karakorum to Cologne), about thirteen thousand kilometres (eight thousand miles), which could take as long as fourteen months. We shall travel across most of Mongolia, ride over the High Altai mountains, cross Kazakhstan, some of Russia, right across the Ukraine, into southern Poland (more mountains – great) and the Czech Republic. I have already made contact with our Embassies in those countries and those countries' Embassies in London, and been offered an amazing amount of help and support. As I write this, I have still not decided whether to buy the Orlov horses or not, the decision largely depends on whether or not I have enough money.

A SELECTION OF OTHER BOXTREE TITLES

❑	0 7522 0219 7	Channel Tunnel Fact File	£4.99 pb
❑	1 85283 479 X	Classic Motorcycles	£12.99 pb
❑	0 7522 1022 X	Classic Ships	£17.99 hb
❑	0 7522 1021 1	Classic Trucks	£12.99 pb
❑	0 7522 1069 6	Coastal Walking	£16.99 hb
❑	0 7522 1026 2	Country Walking	£16.99 hb
❑	1 85283 969 4	Countrywomen	£8.99 pb
❑	0 7522 1054 8	English Arcadia: 100 Years of Country Life	£25.00 hb
❑	1 85283 537 0	Food for Sport	£7.99 pb
❑	1 85283 918 X	Horse Answers	£13.99 pb
❑	0 7522 0551 X	Indonesia	£12.99 pb
❑	1 85283 963 5	Ireland's Wild Countryside	£13.99 pb
❑	1 85283 942 2	It's a Vet's Life	£8.99 pb
❑	0 7522 1091 2	Prehistoric Life	£14.99 pb
❑	0 7522 1602 3	Vienna Walks	£9.99 pb
❑	1 85283 934 1	Waterways	£14.99 hb
❑	0 7522 1623 6	Where to Ski	£14.99 pb

All these books are available at your local bookshop or can be ordered direct from the publisher. Just tick the titles you want and fill in the form, ring 01326 374900, fax the form to 01326 374111, e-mail books©barni.avel.co.uk or post the form to the address below.

Prices and availability subject to change without notice.

Boxtree Cash Sales, P.O. Box 11, Falmouth, Cornwall TR10 9EN

Please send cheque or postal order for the value of the book and add the following for postage and packing:

U.K. including B.F.P.O. – £1.00 for one book, plus 50p for the second book, and 30p for each additional book ordered up to a £3.00 maximum.

Overseas including Eire – £2.00 for the first book, plus £1.00 for the second book, and 50p for each additional book ordered.

OR please debit this amount from my Access/Visa Card (delete as appropriate).

Card Number ☐☐☐☐☐☐☐☐☐☐☐☐☐☐☐☐

Amount £ ....

Expiry Date on card ....

Signed ....

Name ....

Address ....